INTRODUCTION

American history is filled with great women, and so is this book! Discover 84 word search puzzles, each one about a different woman who made history. Every puzzle is paired with a biography. You'll learn about businesswomen like Madam C.J. Walker, the country's first self-made woman millionaire; artists like architect Maya Lin, who designed the Vietnam Veteran's Memorial; and how Sally Ride rocketed into history books with her trip to space. The diverse group featured in this book helped pave the way for women today.

The puzzles follow the familiar format: Every word listed is contained within the letter grid. Words in the list can be found in a straight line horizontally, vertically, or diagonally. Words may read either forward or backward. If you need a hint, answers are found in the back of the book.

One of the most popular ways to tackle a word search is to isolate a letter, scan the lines to find an instance of the letter, then scan the adjoining letters to see if the word can be formed. There are a couple different ways to do this, and puzzle enthusiasts are split on whether it's more helpful to focus on the first letter of the word or on an uncommon letter. Experimentation can help you determine the strategy that works best for you. Likewise, searching for double letters can assist in pinpointing a location.

So sharpen your pencil, test what you know, and learn something new with *Brain Games® Great American Women Word Search*!

ABIGAIL ADAMS

As the wife of president John Adams and the mother of president John Quincy Adams, Abigail Adams (1744–1818) is often considered one of America's founders. She was an early advocate for women's rights, admonishing the Founding Fathers to "remember the ladies" in their new laws. Adams opposed slavery and supported education for women, despite receiving no formal education herself. She was such a close confidante and advisor to her husband that critics called her "Mrs. President." Adams is mainly remembered for the many letters she and her husband wrote to each other, which offer a glimpse of the social and political issues of the time.

ABIGAIL	INDEPENDENCE	REMEMBER
ADAMS	JOHN	REVOLUTION
ADVISOR	LADIES	RIGHTS
ADVOCATE	LAWS	SCHOOL
BELIEFS	LETTERS	SLAVERY
CONFIDANTE	MASSACHUSETTS	UNITED STATES
EDUCATION	MOTHER	VOCAL
FARM	MRS. PRESIDENT	WIFE
FIRST LADY	OPINION	WOMEN
FOUNDER	POLITICS	
GOVERNMENT	QUINCY	

```
I N D E P E N D E N C E E O S G
K T N E D I S E R P S R M S C O
S R E V O L U T I O N L L E I V
S F Z Y R E V A L S E J A I T E
T S E W X H Y C N I U Q C D I R
T E U I D S R O E F P R O A L N
E T Z F L O R V D L O F V L O M
S A G E S E E D U E A U A G P E
U T B I L J B A C T M D N R O N
H S V O O A M N A T O S A D M T
C D R P O B E E T E T J W M E I
A E I I H I M M I R H O Z A S R
S T G N C G E O O S E H J X L Q
S I H I S A R W N U R N N T C U
A N T O J I C O N F I D A N T E
M U S N B L F I R S T L A D Y E
```

Answers on page 172.

JUDITH SARGENT MURRAY

From a young age, Judith Sargent Murray (1751–1820) was aware of the many inequalities faced by women. She began publishing poetry in the 1790s and published a play in 1795. It was likely the first play by an American author produced on stage. She wrote many essays about the importance of women's education and about how the success of the United States as a new nation depended on the intelligence of its citizens–women included. Her landmark essay "On the Equality of the Sexes" was published in 1790.

ACCESS	GLOUCESTER	POETRY
AMERICAN	INCOME	PRODUCED
AUTHOR	INEQUALITY	PSEUDONYM
BOOK	INTELLIGENCE	PUBLISH
BOSTON	JUDITH	SARGENT
DAUGHTER	LITERARY	SEXES
EDUCATION	MAGAZINE	STAGE
EQUALITY	THE MEDIUM	SUCCESS
ESSAY	MURRAY	UNIVERSALISM
FEMALE	NATION	WRITER
THE GLEANER	PLAY	

```
B E L A M E F Y R A R E T I L E
O R E N A E L G E H T P G M F M
S E X E S Y K D A M R N S X A F
T R C I I O T U N O O I J G S R
O E H E O N T I D O L C A M U E
N T S B D H T U L A I Z N T C T
M S I A O U C E S A I T H I C H
Y E L R R E C R L N U E A L E G
N C B I D G E A E L M Q B N S U
O U U T G V E E T E I E E H S A
D O P O I W G N D I S G S N X D
U L U N R A U I T D O S E S I S
E G U I T M U R R A Y N E N A N
S X T S P M H T I D U J V C C Y
P E Q U A L I T Y R T E O P C E
R O U A M E R I C A N Y A L P A
```

Answers on page 172.

MARGARET FULLER

Margaret Fuller (1810–1850) is best known for feminist writing and literary criticism. She advocated for women's rights, education, and employment. Under the strict tutelage of her father, Fuller gained wide learning at an early age. She taught at schools and befriended important intellectuals, including Ralph Waldo Emerson. Beginning in 1839, Fuller held formal group discussions for women, called "Conversations." Fuller became editor of the transcendentalist journal *The Dial* in 1840. She found work at Horace Greeley's *New-York Tribune* in 1844 and published her seminal work *Woman in the Nineteenth Century* in 1845. The *Tribune* sent Fuller to Europe in 1846 as its first female foreign correspondent. She married minor Italian nobleman and fellow revolutionary Giovanni Angelo Ossoli. The couple and their young son perished in a shipwreck in 1850.

ABROAD	EMERSON	NINETEENTH
BEST-READ	FEMINIST	OSSOLI
BIOGRAPHY	FULLER	PAPERS
BOOK	GREELEY	REFORM
CENTURY	HOME	REVOLUTION
CONVERSATIONS	INTELLECTUAL	SHIPWRECK
CRITIC	ITALY	TEACHER
THE DIAL	JOURNAL	TRIBUNE
EDITOR	LITERATURE	
EDUCATION	MARGARET	

```
T Z Y G R E E L E Y D A O R B A
L H U F M K C E R W P I H S H T
H O Q J N L N U P A P E R S S E
M M W N O I T U L O V E R Z N R
E E Y N I N E T E E N T H L O A
O L I T E R A T U R E V W A I G
T T E C B I O G R A P H Y U T R
S E D E L A I D E H T K B T A A
I A U L M T R I B U N E I C S M
N C C C M E E C I T S L L E R R
I H A W I D R T O T B A O L E E
M E T L I T A S R U O N S L V F
E R I T E L I E O F O R S E N O
F F O T Y Y A R B N K U O T O R
G R N M Y D P Y C N J O Z N C M
P S R E L L U F R K B J S I L P
```

Answers on page 172.

SOJOURNER TRUTH

Sojourner Truth was born Isabella Baumfree in New York around 1797. She escaped slavery with her infant daughter in 1826. Shortly thereafter, she successfully sued for the return of her son, who had been illegally sold to a man in Alabama. She became a Methodist, and in 1843 renamed herself Sojourner Truth. While she never learned to read or write, Truth dictated her autobiography–*The Narrative of Sojourner Truth: a Northern Slave* (1850)–to a friend. In 1851, at the Ohio Women's Rights Convention, Truth delivered her famous "Ain't I a Woman?" speech, calling for equal rights for women and African Americans. Truth's clout as a well-known abolitionist helped her recruit Black soldiers for the Union Army during the Civil War. After the war, she advocated for former slaves' property rights. Truth died in 1882. She is remembered as an important abolitionist leader and early advocate of women's rights.

ABOLITIONIST	COURT	NARRATIVE	SOJOURNER
ACTIVIST	EQUALITY	NEW YORK	SPEECH
ADVOCATE	ESCAPE	OHIO	SUFFRAGE
AIN'T	FREEDOM	PREACHER	TEMPERANCE
ARMY	GOVERNMENT	PROPERTY	TROOPS
BLACK	LEADER	RECRUIT	TRUTH
CIVIL WAR	METHODIST	RIGHTS	UNION
CONVENTION	MOVEMENT	SLAVERY	WOMAN

```
T R U T H Y L E Y T T F T Z N L
M P P H S F R M P E N S T O F B
E R R C S I R E M A I I I E R M
V O I E R A N P V V C T A G E O
I P G E E S E O I A N S T A E V
T E H P D R O T I E L R E R D E
A R T S A O C J V T O S U F O M
R T S N E A H N O O I N D F M E
R Y C R L H O I P U I L M U Z N
A E B L A C K S O O R P O S Y T
N C U G O V E R N M E N T B Z R
T S I D O H T E M L A N E N A U
M E Z V R E H C A E R P I R J O
K R O Y W E N Y T I L A U Q E C
T I U R C E R S A D V O C A T E
N A M O W R A W L I V I C A P J
```

Answers on page 172.

HARRIET BEECHER STOWE

Abolitionist author Harriet Beecher Stowe (1811–1896) was heavily influenced by her religious family. In 1836, she met and married Calvin Stowe. He encouraged her writing and the couple had seven children together. When Congress passed the Fugitive Slave Act of 1850, which compelled Northerners to return runaway slaves, Stowe expressed her anger by writing her most famous work, *Uncle Tom's Cabin*. The first installment appeared in an anti-slavery journal in 1851, and was published as a book the next year. The novel is considered a realistic depiction of slavery, and some say that it laid the groundwork for the Civil War.

ABOLITION	FAMILY	RELIGIOUS
ARTICLES	FUGITIVE	RUNAWAY
AUTHOR	HARRIET	SERIAL
BEECHER	INSTALLMENT	SLAVERY
BEST SELLER	JOURNAL	SOUTH
BOOK	MAGAZINE	STOWE
CHILDREN	MOTHER	TOUR
CIVIL WAR	NATIONAL ERA	UNCLE TOM'S CABIN
DEPICTION	NORTHERN	WRITER
EMPATHY	NOVEL	

```
S I F R T R R S R Y A W A N U R
D P A S E E E L U A R H A Y E F
U N M Z I H L E A O W E T I N Q
N D I P R T L V P N I L V U R Y
O I L B R O E O X V R G I A O Y
I G Y M A M S N T E Z U I V L S
T D E A H C T S T O W E O L I S
I E V G O Y S A U T H O R J E C
L P I A T N E M L L A T S N I R
O I T Z A A B R O R E T I R W K
B C I I L G E Y H T A P M E O I
A T G N C H I L D R E N T O U R
W I U E C L A I R E S L B S H W
B O F E J P C B A R T I C L E S
J N E C Q N R E H T R O N N J Z
N B L N A T I O N A L E R A U O
```

Answers on page 173.

ELIZABETH CADY STANTON

Elizabeth Cady Stanton (1815–1902) was an abolitionist and early leader in the women's rights movement. She married abolitionist lecturer Henry Stanton in 1840. While attending the World's Anti-Slavery Convention that year, Stanton met abolitionist Lucretia Mott. Eight years later, Stanton and Mott held the first women's rights convention at Seneca Falls, New York, and penned "The Declaration of Sentiments," proclaiming the equality of the sexes. In the early 1850s, Stanton met Susan B. Anthony and the two struck up a lifelong friendship. The pair established the Women's Loyal National League to campaign for abolishing slavery, published a weekly newspaper called *The Revolution* to lobby for women's rights, and founded the National Woman Suffrage Association.

ABOLITIONIST	FRANCHISE	PROPERTY RIGHTS
ANTHONY	HISTORY	THE REVOLUTION
AUTHOR	LAW	SENECA FALLS
BOOK	LEAGUE	SENTIMENTS
CADY	MOTHER	SPEECH
CONSTITUTION	MOTT	STANTON
CONVENTION	NEW YORK	SUFFRAGE
DECLARATION	OUTSPOKEN	TRAVEL
DIVORCE	PETITION	WOMAN'S BIBLE
ELIZABETH	PRESIDENT	
EQUAL RIGHTS	PROMOTE	

```
O S G T N S E Q U A L R I G H T S F
C P T S N G N J I S P E R O H T U A
W E Q I A H O Q C H T E B A Z I L E
S E C N O P I F B O T A R Y M R N U
E C O O U P T S P E N R N V I F N W
N H N I T R A Y T E C V K T M V O A
E F S T S E R P T O T R E B O Z I L
C R T I P S A J R O R I O N I N T W
A A I L O I L N A Y P Y T V T C U O
F N T O K D C M V Y E R X I I I L M
A C U B E E E O E S N B O Z O D O A
L H T A N N D T L U O O B M O N V N
L I I H S T R T O O G V H B O Z E S
S S O J A Q T A K Z D A L T J T R B
D E N R S T N E M I T N E S N S E I
C A D Y A W S M O T H E R L T A H B
E K P R O P E R T Y R I G H T S T L
P N E W Y O R K D E G A R F F U S E
```

Answers on page 173.

HARRIET TUBMAN

Harriet Tubman was born into slavery in Dorchester County, Maryland, sometime around 1822. Her early life was filled with hardship. Three of her sisters were sold to a distant plantation. She was often beaten and whipped by cruel masters. As an adolescent, Tubman suffered a traumatic head injury when an angry overseer struck her with a two-pound weight, leaving her with a lifetime of severe headaches, seizures, and narcolepsy. Tubman escaped to Philadelphia in 1849. Once free, she immediately returned to Maryland to rescue family members. She became a "conductor" on the Underground Railroad, guiding dozens of slaves to freedom and earning the nickname "Moses." Tubman worked as a cook, nurse, and spy for the Union during the Civil War. She died in 1913, but remains an icon of courage and freedom today.

CIVIL WAR	HARRIET	REWARD
CONDUCTOR	MARYLAND	SCOUT
COOK	MOSES	SLAVERY
DORCHESTER	NETWORK	SPY
ENSLAVED	NURSE	TUBMAN
ESCAPED	PHILADELPHIA	UNDERGROUND
FAMILY	PLANTATION	UNION
FREEDOM	RAILROAD	WEIGHT
GUIDE	RESCUE	

E V I S P D R A W L I V I C R Z
Z S Y L R L N L Z N B X K W O P
M N L A N X A U N L U O H S T Z
O D I V F X D N O A G R N K C P
S E M E R E O A T R M Q S C U O
E V A R E U R I D A G B Z E D M
S A F Y E C C H M A T R U L N F
E L A E D S H P A B O I E T O G
X S M I O E E L R F G R O D C U
F N P P M R S E Y W U D L N N W
D E B B B U T D L K E Z P I S U
E U N I O N E A A T E I R R A H
D R A W E R R L N O K U G Y H R
N E T W O R K I D G O Q L H P I
O U E D I U G H T U O C S W T S
D E P A C S E P B I C X G H Q P

Answers on page 173.

17

CLARA BARTON

A shy and timid child, Clara Barton (1821–1912) preferred reading to socializing. Barton first found her calling to help others when she nursed her brother back to health after an accident. She worked as a teacher for more than a decade. During the Civil War she worked for the Union Army and eventually became a nurse, earning the nickname "Angel of the Battlefield." After visiting Europe and working for the International Red Cross during the Franco-Prussian War of 1870–1871, Barton sought to open an American branch of the Red Cross. The American Red Cross was founded in 1881, and Barton served as its first president. However, she never took a salary for her work in the organization.

AMERICAN	EDUCATOR	RELIEF
ANGEL	EUROPE	SCHOOL
ARMY	HUMANITARIAN	SHY
BARTON	INTERNATIONAL	SOLDIERS
BATTLEFIELD	LECTURE	TIMID
BROTHER	MILITIA	UNION
CARE	NURSE	WAR
CLARA	PRESIDENT	
CLARISSA	RED CROSS	

```
O K P T K M K A M P C T J O Z E
P N F C N P G E R A K U A H U W
V D H S L E I W R M L V N R T Z
A C L A R A D E K E Y O O I O E
A D H A M E R I C A N P O I O P
N F L U Z Z I I S J E T U H V N
G E U E M N B D S E F H F S C N
E I J R I A W J L S R S H Y O S
L L B D E F N D N O A P Q T R Q
Z E T T K D E I I M S S R A E K
E R G W V R C L T X I A W V S Y
T I M I D X I R T A B L K B R Z
R E H T O R B P O T R G I S U O
U L E C T U R E Y S A I T T N W
N S R O T A C U D E S B A J I D
L A N O I T A N R E T N I N M A
```

Answers on page 173.

LOUISA MAY ALCOTT

Raised among famous intellectuals like Ralph Waldo Emerson and Henry David Thoreau, Louisa May Alcott (1832–1888) was inspired to write from a young age. Alcott was taught mostly by her father and her literary neighbors. From an early age, she worked as a teacher and domestic servant, among other positions, to help financially support her struggling family. By 1851, Alcott was regularly publishing poems and short stories, writing under a pen name. Alcott's accounts of her Civil War experiences, *Hospital Sketches* (1863), confirmed her desire to pursue writing more seriously. In 1869, Alcott published *Little Women*, which brought her fame and financial independence. The novel contains many autobiographical details of Alcott's life with her three sisters. Alcott was a feminist and abolitionist throughout her life.

ALCOTT	HOSPITAL	PEN NAME
A.M. BARNARD	JO'S BOYS	POEMS
AUTHOR	LITTLE MEN	PSEUDONYM
BOOKS	LITTLE WOMEN	SERVANT
CHARACTERS	LOUISA MAY	SHORT STORIES
EMERSON	MAGAZINE	SISTERS
FAMILY	NEW ENGLAND	TEACHER
FEMINIST	NOVELS	THOREAU
FLORA FAIRFIELD	NURSE	WRITER

```
G T A D B Y N N C A H H K N E R
F U S O N O L S R O T S G E M E
C L O I S A E I S M E R M M A T
F K O R N R L P M I K O P O N I
S Q E R V I I G R A G H S W N R
M M Z A A T M O N C F T E E E W
E A N A A F T E H E R U U L P S
Y T G L M S A A F E W A D T N I
H A Z A T B R I H M N E O T E S
N N M R Z A A C R O S X N I M T
D U O A C I A R V F E Q Y L E E
O H R T S E N E N B I P M P L R
S C E S T I L E M A P E O H T S
B R B X E S U A J H R E L D T K
S D C J O S B O Y S M D W D I R
U A E R O H T O L S T T O C L A
```

Answers on page 174.

SUSAN B. ANTHONY

Raised in the Quaker faith, Susan B. Anthony (1820–1906) grew up with the belief that everyone was equal under God. This idea guided her to become an activist and abolitionist. She gave speeches against slavery, even risking arrest in the process. In 1851, she met Elizabeth Cady Stanton at an anti-slavery conference. The pair established the American Equal Rights Association in 1866, began publishing *The Revolution*, a weekly paper advocating for women's rights, in 1868, and founded the National Woman Suffrage Association in 1869. Anthony even illegally voted in the 1872 presidential election, for which she was fined $100, but never paid. For her many efforts, she was honored with the Susan B. Anthony dollar coin in 1979–making her the first female citizen to be depicted on U.S. coinage.

ABOLITIONIST	LEADER	SOCIETY
ACTIVIST	LECTURE	SPEECHES
ANTHONY	NATIONAL	STANTON
ASSOCIATION	NEW YORK	SUFFRAGE
AUTHOR	NEWSPAPER	SUSAN
COIN	POLITICS	TEACHER
DOLLAR	PUBLISH	TEMPERANCE
EQUAL	QUAKER	TOUR
FINED	THE REVOLUTION	VOTED
FOUNDER	RIGHTS	WOMAN
FRIEND	SLAVERY	

```
S L F L A S S O C I A T I O N N
E N A R A D E N I F O I Q X S E
H J Z U I N N R E H C A E T O W
C P N H Q E O A C Q V O R E C S
E E O G T E N I S O T E I C I P
E M I L S S F D T U D R U N E A
P A T O I S I E R A S A H A T P
S Q U Q N T D V E I N L S R Y E
A E L Q O A I L I N M L I E E R
U G O U I N F C P T H O L P R I
T A V A T T O G S G C D B M U R
H R E K I O U R U O T A U E T I
O F R E L N N N A M O W P T C G
R F E R O R D Y N O H T N A E H
Z U H R B F E S L A V E R Y L T
U S T N A V R A N E W Y O R K S
```

Answers on page 174.

JULIA WARD HOWE

The daughter of a New York banker and a poet, Julia Ward Howe (1819–1910) was a well-read child. As an adult, Howe pursued her love of writing and often used it to criticize traditional women's roles, which caused friction in her marriage. Howe wrote her best-known work after a visit to Washington, D.C., during the Civil War. She noticed the soldiers singing a marching song called "John Brown's Body," and decided to write some new lyrics for the tune. Her poem became the "Battle Hymn of the Republic," which was published in the *Atlantic Monthly* in 1862. It became a rallying cry not only for the Civil War, but for the abolitionist and suffrage movements. After the war, Howe established and led many women's organizations and became a peace activist.

ABOLITIONIST

ACTIVIST

ANTHEM

BATTLE

CIVIL WAR

HOWE

HYMN

JOURNAL

JULIA

LYRICS

MOVEMENT

PACIFIST

PASSION-FLOWERS

PEACE

POEM

PUBLISH

RALLYING CRY

REFORMER

REPUBLIC

SOCIAL

SONG

SUFFRAGE

UNION

WARD

WOMAN

WRITING

```
R W R I T I N G J N A M O W L S
X E R X X W A M L O M G A O R C
O M M K H O W E L C U I C E M I
A E S R S M O H A T L R W Q Y R
Y B E O O A U T J U S O N U K Y
R M O L N F M N J L L K N A R L
C O Y L T G E A Z F M I T N L V
G V X V I T K R N P O S U C I E
N E C A M T A O U N I R I I T G
I M I W U I I B P F V V F S C A
Y E L C Y S L O I N I W I E K R
L N B T S I M C N L Z V H C Q F
L T U A S W A E W I I B Y A K F
A N P H S P A A O T S W M E V U
R C E D X P R R C P B T N P I S
N A R J V M Q A D S O C I A L I
```

Answers on page 174.

VICTORIA WOODHULL

Victoria Woodhull (1838–1927) was born into an eclectic family. Woodhull and her sister, Tennessee, were involved in the spiritual community of clairvoyance and fortune-telling. In 1868, the sisters moved to New York City, where they met and provided psychic services to Cornelius Vanderbilt. The wealthy Vanderbilt was impressed with the sisters and helped them set up the first woman-owned stockbrokerage firm. In 1872, Woodhull became the first woman to run for president of the United States under the newly-formed Equal Rights Party. She was an advocate for women's rights and the freedom to marry, divorce, and bear children without government restrictions.

ACTIVIST	FREEDOM	SPIRITUAL
BROKERAGE	HISTORY	SUFFRAGE
BUSINESS	MARRIAGE	TENNESSEE
CLAIRVOYANCE	NEW YORK CITY	VANDERBILT
DIVORCE	NEWSPAPER	VICTORIA
ELECTION	POLITICS	WALL STREET
EQUAL RIGHTS	PRESIDENT	WEALTH
FIRM	PSYCHIC	WOODHULL
FORTUNE	REFORM	
FREE LOVE	SISTER	

```
N O I T C E L E B M R O F E R T
S C E Q U A L R I G H T S T T L
U L H I S T O R Y Z L M N B W I
F G L Q W K C A O Z N E E U A B
F A K U E I I M B E D N C S L R
R C N R H R O E W I U I R I L E
A S A C O D V Y S T V R O N S D
G G Y T E O O E R W K M V E T N
E S C E L R R O I A E T I S R A
P I R E K P F H W V I A D S E V
V F E C N A Y O V R I A L C E P
R R I M V E E S S E N N E T T J
F T R Y R E P A P S W E N J H J
Y I U E G A I R R A M S G X F J
F S P I R I T U A L R E T S I S
S C I T I L O P A C T I V I S T
```

Answers on page 174.

EMILY DICKINSON

Emily Dickinson (1830–1886) began writing as a teenager and was considered an exceptionally bright student. After slipping into a deep depression after the death of a friend, Dickinson began to live an isolated life. Some scholars say she suffered from depression, agoraphobia, or possibly epilepsy. Although she wrote nearly 1,800 poems throughout her life, fewer than 12 were published during her lifetime. She is known for her unique style that was unlike the conventional poetry of her era.

ACADEMY	GARDEN	POSTHUMOUS
AMHERST	INFLUENCE	PUBLISHED
CARLO	ISOLATION	STOP
COLLECTION	LETTERS	STUDENT
DEATH	LIFE	SUSAN
DICKINSON	MASSACHUSETTS	THEMES
DOG	MASTER	UNUSUAL
ECCENTRIC	MUSEUM	VOLUME
EMILY	NATURE	WOMAN IN WHITE
FLOWERS	NEW ENGLAND	
FRIENDSHIP	POETRY	

```
K S O N O I T A L O S I G R U S
R R N S N E W E N G L A N D C T
E E P A U S U O M U H T S O P O
F W T O T S T U D E N T S D C P
R O E S E U A G O D C T Z O U I
I L F T A T R N N A T A L H N M
E F P B I M R E C E M L R F H U
N C D U W H D Y S A E H L L L S
D T I O B R W U L C C U E E O E
S H C R A L H N T A E A T R E U
H E K G T C I I I N U T D V S M
I M I I A N O S C N E S O E I T
P E N S B N E E H R A L U E M B
T S S X Z Q T C S E U M F N A Y
B A O D E A T H C M D I O F U B
M W N E M I L Y E E L H D W B V
```

Answers on page 175.

MARY CASSATT

Mary Cassatt (1844–1926) was born into a relatively well-to-do family that valued travel and education. At age 15, Cassatt enrolled at the Pennsylvania Academy of Fine Arts. Frustrated with sexist instruction and attitudes there, she moved to Paris in 1866 to continue her studies. In 1868, one of Cassatt's paintings was accepted at the Paris Salon, an annual art exhibition. In 1877, Edgar Degas invited Cassatt to join an independent group of artists known as the Impressionists. Cassatt often painted scenes from the lives of women, with particular emphasis on the bond between mother and child. Cassatt's eyesight began failing in the early 1900s, eventually forcing her to give up painting. Cassatt was an outspoken advocate of women's rights, and she resented being stereotyped as a "woman artist."

ACADEMY	EUROPE	MOTHERS
AMERICAN	EXHIBITION	OPERA
ARTIST	EYESIGHT	PAINTER
BOATING PARTY (The)	FAMILY	PARIS
CANVAS	FRANCE	PENNSYLVANIA
CAREER	GROUP	PORTRAITS
CASSATT	IMPRESSIONISTS	STUDY
CHILD'S BATH (The)	LOUVRE	SUBJECTS
CHILDREN	MARY	THEATER
DEGAS	MASTERS	WOMEN

```
Y R S O P U O R G R E U R O P E
L E T P N C R P E L Y S A G E D
I T S E N U Y E Y O M S H W W P
M A I R B E T J N U E R T E P E
A E N A X T R E V V D E A X A N
F H O A A P M D Y R A T B H I N
P T I S C O A R L E C S S I N S
S C S C W I A R P I A A D B T Y
T A S U A M R O I T H M L I E L
C N E Z U R R E H S K C I T R V
E V R M F T E G M W E S H I V A
J A P C R Y I E O A I C C O D N
B S M A D S T N R H Z N N N D I
U P I U E R Z Z T S I T R A B A
S T T Y S R E H T O M Y C S R J
S S E B O A T I N G P A R T Y F
```

Answers on page 175.

JANE ADDAMS

After graduating at the top of her class from Rockford Female Seminary and then briefly studying medicine, Jane Addams (1860–1935) found her true calling in 1888. On a trip to London with her friend Ellen Gates Starr, Addams visited Toynbee Hall, a settlement house that provided social services to the poor. In 1889, Addams and Starr founded Hull House in Chicago, which provided day care, job training, and English classes to thousands of people a week. Outside her role as a social reformer, Addams was a deeply committed pacifist and peace activist. For her efforts, she was awarded the Nobel Peace Prize in 1931–the first American woman to win that honor.

ACLU	HULL HOUSE	POOR
ACTIVIST	ILLINOIS	PRESIDENT
ADDAMS	JANE	REFORMER
AMERICAN	JOB TRAINING	SEMINARY
AWARD	JUSTICE	SERVICES
BOOK	LECTURER	SOCIAL WORK
CHARITIES	LONDON	TOYNBEE
CHICAGO	NAACP	WAR
CLASSES	NOBEL	WOMAN
COFOUNDER	PACIFIST	
EDUCATION	PEACE	

```
W  B  E  P  R  I  L  L  I  N  O  I  S  H  K  Z
T  H  O  S  R  E  F  O  R  M  E  R  P  A  G  N
P  O  M  W  U  H  W  A  V  W  K  T  E  Q  T  H
R  E  D  N  U  O  F  O  C  O  O  O  D  R  N  R
E  I  A  P  Z  N  H  S  M  L  H  Y  U  Y  E  L
C  C  P  C  A  J  E  L  R  A  U  N  C  R  D  E
I  V  H  A  E  C  O  T  L  K  N  B  A  A  I  C
T  L  C  A  I  T  S  B  R  U  V  E  T  N  S  T
S  P  O  V  R  I  N  O  T  D  H  E  I  I  E  U
U  E  R  N  F  I  W  A  G  R  R  J  O  M  R  R
J  E  S  I  D  L  T  A  C  A  A  D  N  E  P  E
S  R  C  S  A  O  D  I  H  I  C  I  R  S  P  R
B  A  A  I  A  D  N  E  E  H  R  I  N  A  Z  R
P  O  C  W  A  L  N  C  L  S  W  E  H  I  W  X
U  O  O  M  H  A  C  L  E  B  O  N  M  C  N  A
S  T  S  K  J  T  S  I  V  I  T  C  A  A  H  G
```

Answers on page 175.

NELLIE BLY

Nellie Bly (1864–1922) began her writing career as a teenager when she penned a response to a demeaning column published in the *Pittsburgh Dispatch* entitled "What Girls Are Good For." The newspaper's editor was so impressed with Bly's rebuttal that he offered her a job. Two years later, Bly moved to New York City and began working for the *New York World*. In one of her first assignments for the *World*, Bly spent several days posing as a mental patient for an exposé entitled "Ten Days in a Mad-House," in which she uncovered the deplorable conditions of the Women's Lunatic Asylum on Blackwell's Island. Her other career-defining assignment came in 1889, when the paper sent her on a trip around the world in a record-setting 72 days. Bly is remembered as a pioneer of investigative journalism.

ASSIGNMENT	INVESTIGATE	PEN NAME
ASYLUM	ISLAND	PIONEER
BLACKWELL'S	JOURNALISM	PITTSBURGH
BLY	JOURNEY	RECORD
CAREER	MAD-HOUSE	TRAVEL
COLUMNIST	NELLIE	WORLD
DAYS	NEW YORK	WRITER
DISPATCH	NEWSPAPER	
EXPOSÉ	PATIENT	

```
G N S P J O U R N A L I S M R P
J U U O U S H N J B M U L Y S A
O B H G D Y B L A C K W E L L S
U P R E P A P S W E N Y R Z T E
R V M D H D P X M E X P O S E M
N T I I Q C W I L A E C I M H A
E P N J N O T D A D N D O L N
Y I E E R V N A Q T M H V A V N
Q O G L M A E O P U S C O L Y E
P N D V L N P S L S L B E U J P
A E E S D B G O T C I V U F S T
T E I D R L C I J I A D Z R T E
I R L M O Y L E S R G R A V G F
E W L N C S S R T S C A E H S H
N W E R E T I R W M A V T E Q Q
T E N P R N E W Y O R K L E R G
```

Answers on page 175.

IDA B. WELLS

Born into slavery in Mississippi, Ida B. Wells (1862–1931) was freed at a young age by the Emancipation Proclamation. At age 16, after yellow fever killed both her parents and a younger sibling, Wells dropped out of school and took a job as a teacher to support her other siblings. In 1882, Wells moved her siblings to Memphis, where she began to work as a journalist. After the lynching of a friend by a White mob, Wells began to investigate lynchings and publish her findings in local newspapers and pamphlets. Enraged locals burned her newspaper press to the ground, so she moved to Chicago where she became the first paid African American correspondent for a major White newspaper. Wells went on to help establish several civil rights organizations, most notably the National Association for the Advancement of Colored People (NAACP).

ACTIVIST	JOURNALIST	PAMPHLETS
BARNETT	LAWSUIT	PRESS
CAMPAIGN	LYNCHING	PUBLISHER
CHICAGO	MEMPHIS	RECONSTRUCTION
CIVIL RIGHTS	MISSISSIPPI	RESEARCHER
CORRESPONDENT	MOB	SIBLINGS
FREE SPEECH	NAACP	TEACHER
IDA	NEWSPAPER	TRAIN
IOLA	OWNER	WELLS

```
P R E S S S I B L I N G S R O H
C R C O R R E S P O N D E N T J
H N T S I V I T C A F C M S R Y
S C P C V L O D R L O L I L E T
H B I I A G P E Q N M J S L H T
P C O V A M P C S Y O L S E S E
T L E C I A P T A U B A I W I N
A E I E P L R A R A S W S L L R
O H A S P U R N I I N S S Y B A
C C W C C S A I H G O U I N U B
S E I T H L E P G W N I P C P R
N O I D I E M E N H D T P H A I
D O Z S A E R E R X T V I I U N
N H T V M T R H M F Q S L N L X
P A M P H L E T S H L E I G H K
M R E H C R A E S E R T R A I N
```

Answers on page 176.

SUSAN LA FLESCHE

Susan La Flesche (1865–1915) grew up on Nebraska's Omaha reservation. As a girl, she watched an American Indian woman die because a White doctor refused to come treat her. This motivated La Flesche to become a doctor herself. She attended the Woman's Medical College of Pennsylvania, and became the first female Native American to earn a medical degree. She returned to her reservation and became the sole doctor for the territory, often working 20-hour days. La Flesche spoke out against the evils of alcohol, preached hygiene and prevention, and advocated for the Omaha to manage their own land. She married Henry Picotte and had two children, but continued her medical practice. From medical school onward, La Flesche campaigned to build a hospital on the reservation. It finally opened in 1913 and was later renamed in her honor.

ALCOHOL	INDIAN	REFORMER
AMERICAN	LA FLESCHE	RESERVATION
CAMPAIGN	MEDICAL	SUSAN
DEGREE	NATIVE	TEMPERANCE
DOCTOR	OMAHA	TRIBE
FIRST	PHYSICIAN	TRUST
HEALTH	PICOTTE	TUBERCULOSIS
HOSPITAL	PRACTICE	
HOUSE CALL	PUBLIC	

```
H A T B E H C S E L F A L C C D
Y T H N A T I V E D K W M I N E
M R E S E R V A T I O N X A Y G
P X C A M P A I G N E C S B Y R
P R A C T I C E N P S U T F E E
H T U B E R C U L O S I S O C E
T X E T T O C I P A I N M N R T
L E C D I W D S Q D T E A A E J
A L L A C E S U O H D I M M C Q
E L O H O C L A I I C E P C T W
H E O V Z A W I C I R E I S T W
X B M R Y C N A S I R L U S O H
Y I A G G D L Y C A B R R Z R H
R R H F I R H A N U T I I S I N
P T A A S P N C P X F M Q F N T
R V N L S R E M R O F E R A T Q
```

Answers on page 176.

EDITH WHARTON

Edith Jones Wharton (1862-1937) was raised in an upper class New York family. The saying "keeping up with the Joneses" is said to refer to her father's family. Wharton began writing as a teenager, publishing poems and novellas anonymously or under pseudonyms. An avid gardener and interior designer, her first major published work was 1897's *The Decoration of Houses*. She designed her own house, The Mount, which still stands in Lenox, Massachusetts. Wharton's greatest success would be her 1920 novel *The Age of Innocence*, for which she became the first woman to win the Pulitzer Prize for literature. She eventually settled in France, divorced her husband of almost 30 years, and found a place in the intellectual circles of artists and writers in Paris. Wharton is considered one of America's greatest writers.

AGE OF INNOCENCE (The)	JONESES	REEF (The)
ARISTOCRACY	LENOX	SOCIETY
DECORATION	LITERATURE	STORIES
DESIGN	NEW YORK	THE MOUNT
EDITH	NON-FICTION	TOUCHSTONE (The)
ETHAN FROME	NOVELLA	TRAVEL
FAMILY	NOVELS	UPPER CLASS
GILDED AGE	PARIS	VERSES
GLIMPSES OF THE MOON (The)	POEMS	WHARTON
	PRIZE	WRITER
HOUSE OF MIRTH (The)	PUBLISH	YALE
	PULITZER	

```
Y L I M A F K R O Y W E N U S S I S
X B Q O Y T E I C O S D K L Y N G Y
D T L I T E R A T U R E E C L L X C
E K C H X P D D N T W V A E I S L L
S S M E O P U R L J O R N M P A E F
I S F N S U A L O N C O P U U G V N
G A E N O W S N I O X S K T B E A O
N L A M R I E E T T E R O W L O R N
Y C T I O S T S O S Z U I G I F T F
P R T N E R I A O F C E I X S I S I
V E N S U R F F R H M L R K H N E C
R P R N A O T N S O D I L D W N I T
P P Y Z O H M T A E C S R H E O R I
R U B A E V O E D H E E A T E C O O
I D J M L N E A H S T R D D H E T N
Z L O P E E G L R T T E I U V N S I
E O P R E E F E L O D T X M I C C M
N S I R A P V F N A H P X W A E K P
```

Answers on page 176.

MADAM C.J. WALKER

Madam C.J. Walker (1867–1919) rose from poverty in the South to become a self-made millionaire. Born Sarah Breedlove on a Louisiana plantation, she was orphaned at a young age, married as a teenager, and widowed with a two-year-old daughter at age 20. Suffering from a scalp disorder that caused her to lose much of her hair, Breedlove developed her own hair care formula. She married ad-man Charles J. Walker, renamed herself Madam C.J. Walker, and launched her own line of products for African American hair. Her business flourished and she became the wealthiest self-made woman in the U.S. at the time. Walker was also known for her philanthropy and activism.

ACTIVIST	FACTORY	SALES
ADVANCEMENT	FORMULA	SARAH
BEAUTY SCHOOL	HAIR	SELF-MADE
BREEDLOVE	HARLEM	ST. LOUIS
BUSINESS	INDIANAPOLIS	TRAINING
COMPANY	MADAM	VILLA LEWARO
COSMETICS	NEW YORK	WALKER
DENVER	PHILANTHROPY	YMCA
EDUCATION	PRODUCTS	
ENTREPRENEUR	RENAISSANCE	

Y R O T C A F I Y Y N A P M O C
G W A L K E R D E N V E R S O Q
B E A U T Y S C H O O L S N R E
P R W R P B K R O Y W E N L A D
H U G E T R A I N I N G F D W U
I E H N A E O H A I R O V A E C
L N R A S E A D S C R A C E L A
A E T I R D X U U M N O J X A T
N R M S H L B D U C S N A R L I
T P A S A O E L E M T C V G L O
H E D A R V A M E S M S Y W I N
R R A N A E E T E Y C K I U V F
O T M C S N I L T S I V I T C A
P N V E T C A P E D A M F L E S
Y E I F S S S T L O U I S U J Z
S I L O P A N A I D N I X Y G O

Answers on page 176.

MARY MCLEOD BETHUNE

Mary McLeod Bethune (1875–1955) was born to former slaves in South Carolina, the 15th of 17 children. With the help of benefactors, she was able to obtain an education that was never afforded to her parents. After graduating Scotia Seminary (now Barber-Scotia College) in 1893, Bethune studied at Dwight Moody's Institute for Home and Foreign Missions (now Moody Bible Institute) in Chicago. She then returned to the South and began her teaching career. Believing that education was the key to racial advancement, Bethune founded a school for African American girls in Florida in 1904. Bethune was elected president of the National Association of Colored Women's Clubs, became the founding president of the National Council of Negro Women, and served as an advisor to President Franklin D. Roosevelt.

ADVISOR	ELECTED	PRESIDENT
BETHUNE	EQUALITY	ROOSEVELT
CHICAGO	FLORIDA	SCHOOL
CLUB	FOUNDER	SCOTIA
COLLEGE	GRADUATE	SEMINARY
COUNCIL	LEARN	SOUTH CAROLINA
DAYTONA	MARY	STUDENTS
DONORS	MCLEOD	STUDY
EDUCATION	MOODY'S	TEACHER

```
P H K T R S R O O S E V E L T O
G R A D U A T E E Z S M H Y D S
Y E E E G E L L O C Q P W N O O
S D D S Y D O O M N S Y L B N U
S C U U I T D A Y T O N A C O T
T S O T C D I M U D W Z A C R H
A C L T S A E L E Q K D O A S C
J H M U I F T N A B Q U W F T A
D O J Z B A U I T U N V O B N R
E O B B Y H D R O C Q U G D E O
T L P U T M E V I N N E A O D L
C E L E L H A L I D L I C E U I
E A B Y C C Y R E S I H I L T N
L R J A L O P R Y H O D H C S A
E N E Y R A N I M E S R C M L I
W T A D I R O L F C C E A N K D
```

Answers on page 177.

HELEN KELLER

At 19 months of age, Helen Keller (1880–1968) contracted a mysterious illness that left her both deaf and blind. Keller developed her own crude system of gestures to communicate with family; however, she often vented frustrations through tantrums. With the help of teacher Anne Sullivan, Keller eventually learned fingerspelling, braille, and how to speak and understand other people's speech using the Tadoma method, sometimes called tactile lipreading. The two women worked together for 49 years. Keller went on to earn a college degree from Radcliffe College of Harvard University, write several books, and become a prominent member of the Socialist Party of America. She campaigned for women's suffrage and labor rights, helped found the American Civil Liberties Union (ACLU), and advocated for blind people around the world.

ACLU	FINGERSPELLING	SIGN
ALABAMA	FOUNDATION	SOCIALIST
BLIND	HELEN	SPEAK
BOOKS	HUMANITARIAN	SUFFRAGE
BRAILLE	KELLER	SULLIVAN
CAMBRIDGE	LABOR	TADOMA
COLLEGE	LECTURE	TOUR
COMMUNICATE	MEMOIR	WATER
DEAF	PERKINS	WRITER
DEGREE	RADCLIFFE	
EDUCATION	RIGHTS	

```
B W E R U T C E L B S E X S R T
M R E Z H Z Y S L U L T I F N S
D I F T D T R I O L S G H O R U
N T F O D E N O I C N X I G X F
N E I U E D G A B N I T K O I F
O R L R A G R R A A A A E D C R
I C C E F B E V E D L D L O Z A
T T D X H T I K N E Q C L I Y G
A M A B A L A U U H A L E Y S E
C R R W L C O X J L E M R W T T
U I S U L F H Z M G C B O O K S
D O S S N I K R E P A A W D F E
E M E G D I R B M A C S P E A K
F E H U M A N I T A R I A N M T
H M V X Y C O M M U N I C A T E
I U G N I L L E P S R E G N I F
```

Answers on page 177.

MARY PICKFORD

Silent film star Mary Pickford (1892–1979) was known as "American's Sweetheart" long before Julia Roberts or Jennifer Lawrence. Pickford starred in 52 feature films throughout her career, including hits like *Poor Little Rich Girl* and *Pollyanna*. She worked as a producer, as well. In 1919, Pickford cofounded the film company United Artists, along with D.W. Griffith, Charlie Chaplin, and Douglas Fairbanks. In 1929, Pickford starred in her first talking picture, *Coquette*, for which she won an Oscar for Best Actress. Unfortunately, her talkies were never as popular as her silent films, and she made her last movie in 1933. Pickford's business savvy made her a pioneer for women in the early days of film, and she remained on the board of directors of United Artists for many years.

ACADEMY

ACTING

ACTRESS

AUDITION

BILLING

CALIFORNIA

CHAPLIN

COFOUNDER

COMPANY

COQUETTE

CURLS

FAIRBANKS

FILM

GRIFFITH

HOLLYWOOD

INGENUE

LEGENDARY

MARY

MOTION PICTURE

OSCAR

PICKFORD

POLLYANNA

POOR LITTLE RICH GIRL

PRODUCER

SILENT

STAR

SWEETHEART

TALKIE

UNITED ARTISTS

```
H F T N R U A J R Q P R O D U C E R
L R I G H C I R E L T T I L R O O P
B P V L Q F N Z K P I C K F O R D N
A S J T M A R P C O F O U N D E R L
U I W E P I O R S W E E T H E A R T
Y L Z T X R F W R A C T R E S S E M
A E H T C B I G Z M L Y U Z T R P I
L N T E Z A L S E B N B Z S U O N P
E T I U A N A O T A U E I T L G M K
G M F Q U K C H P A I T C L E R K N
E G F O D S A M J K R I Y N L Y U N
N H I C I C O L L A P A U M S I M C
D A R W T C M A D N N E N I A F N M
A N G I I B T E O N H P B U H R E G
R T N O O M T I A R A C S O T G Y Q
Y G N C N I T Q H T N I L P A H C A
U D U I N O D O O W Y L L O H G Q W
R I Y U M K E J Y M E D A C A K L I
```

Answers on page 177.

MARGARET SANGER

Margaret Sanger (1879–1966) was an early feminist and lifelong advocate for women's reproductive rights. Sanger was raised in a poor household with 10 siblings. She became a nurse, married, and had three children. In 1910, Sanger moved to the Manhattan neighborhood of Greenwich Village and became involved in leftist politics. Sanger campaigned for sex education and worked as a nurse on New York City's Lower East Side. After treating a number of women who had undergone dangerous back-alley abortions, she started a publication promoting a woman's right to birth control (a term she coined), which violated the Comstock Act. In 1916, Sanger opened the first birth control clinic in the United States. In 1921, she founded the American Birth Control League, a precursor to today's Planned Parenthood. Later in life, she spearheaded the effort that resulted in the modern birth control pill.

ACTIVIST	JAIL	PUBLICATION
ADVOCATE	LABOR STRIKE	RAID
BIRTH CONTROL	LEAGUE	REFORMER
CLINIC	LOWER EAST SIDE	REPRODUCTION
COMSTOCK ACT	MARGARET	SANGER
CONTRACEPTION	MOTHER	SEX EDUCATION
COURT	NEW YORK	SOCIALISM
FAMILY PLANNING	NURSE	UNION
FEMINIST	PILL	WOMEN
GREENWICH	POLITICS	

```
N B I R T H C O N T R O L I N N
J O T E F R E C I N I L C O W O
E E F G A E U F E M I N I S T I
K D I N M P G L L I P T M M J T
I I E A I R A I Y N P J S A G A
R S T S L O E A B E S R I R R C
T T A T Y D L J C W D E L G E I
S S C R P U Y A A Y S F A A E L
R A O U L C R E C O C O I R N B
O E V O A T R S T R I R C E W U
B R D C N I E R I K T M O T I P
A E A O N O H U V P I E S W C E
L W C Y I N T N I H L R L R H K
W O M E N C O M S T O C K A C T
N L D L G B M B T N P U N I O N
Q N O I T A C U D E X E S D O M
```

Answers on page 177.

GEORGIA O'KEEFFE

Georgia O'Keeffe (1887–1986) knew by age 10 that she wanted to be an artist. She attended the Art Institute of Chicago and the Art Students League in New York City. While teaching at Columbia College in South Carolina, O'Keeffe began a series of charcoal drawings, which she mailed to her friend, Anita Pollitzer. Pollitzer, in turn, showed the drawings to influential art dealer Alfred Stieglitz, who exhibited her work at his gallery, 291. O'Keeffe and Stieglitz continued working together, and eventually married. By the 1920s, she was the highest paid American woman artist. O'Keeffe was awarded the Presidential Medal of Freedom in 1977, and the National Medal of Arts in 1985. O'Keeffe is best known for her paintings of flowers, animal skulls, and New Mexico landscapes. She is often called the "Mother of American Modernism."

AMERICAN	FLOWERS	ORIENTAL POPPIES
ART DEALER	GALLERY	PAINTER
ARTIST	GEORGIA	POLLITZER
BLACK IRIS	LANDSCAPE	RED CANNA
CANVAS	MEDAL	SKULLS
CHARCOAL	MODERNISM	SKYSCRAPERS
CHICAGO	MUSEUM	SOUTHWESTERN
COLUMBIA	NEW MEXICO	STIEGLITZ
DRAWINGS	O'KEEFE	TEACHER

```
R E T N I A P D R A W I N G S F
S L A N D S C A P E E F E E K O
R E Q E M O G A C I H C U P X I
A P I D N R E T S E W H T U O S
F N O P O S K Y S C R A P E R S
L B N L P C A S F A Z Z C B W T
O S B A L O I I K A H X A L M E
W A T A C I P X G U T O N A O A
E L I I M D T L E R L U V C D C
R A G B E E E Z A M O L A K E H
S O A M M G R R E T W E S I R E
L C L U S U L I S R N E G R N R
A R L S O G L I C U T E N I I J
D A E E U S T O T A W Q I S S J
E H R U A R W R C Z N H D R M A
M C Y M A R E L A E D T R A O Q
```

Answers on page 178.

AMELIA EARHART

As a child, Amelia Earhart (1897–1937) compiled a scrapbook of newspaper clippings of women in male-oriented fields. In 1920, Earhart took a 10-minute plane ride while visiting an airfield, and decided then she wanted to learn to fly. She saved up money for flying lessons, and became the 16th woman issued a pilot's license. In 1928, Earhart was offered the opportunity to be the first woman to fly across the Atlantic Ocean. Earhart succeeded, albeit as a passenger, and became an instant celebrity. In 1932, she became the first woman to fly solo across the Atlantic as a pilot. Earhart continued making solo flights and set seven women's aviation records between 1930 and 1935. In 1937, she began the first around-the-world-flight at the equator. After completing over 22,000 miles, Earhart disappeared. She has never been found, despite extensive search efforts.

AIRFIELD	EARHART	PILOT
ALTITUDE	FEMALE	PLANE
AMELIA	FIRST	PUBLICITY
ATLANTIC	FLIGHT	PUTNAM
AVIATION	LADY LINDY	RECORDS
AWARD	LESSONS	SCRAPBOOK
CELEBRITY	LICENSE	SHOW
CROSS	MEDIA	SOLO
DISAPPEARED	NAVIGATOR	WOMAN

```
V S O L O P L A N E V A S U O Y
K K O O B P A R C S L H F R R T
P A I D E M D V H T O L I P W A
S D C Y O L I A I W J Q R H R D
N I I T H L P T U A N P S X R R
O S B I P A U L R M T J T A L O
S A Q R C D B A U A A I W Z U T
S P E B E Y L N K N H A O J A A
E P S E Y L I T E T S R W N P G
L E N L Z I C I M U E C A K V I
Q A E E X N I C W P U A K E R V
B R C C V D T O O E L A M E F A
O E I K J Y Y A M E L I A C W N
L D L Z H Q D Q A J F L I G H T
D L E I F R I A N B F X D C O W
F X F S S O R C S D R O C E R K
```

Answers on page 178.

PEARL BUCK

Born to Presbyterian missionaries in West Virginia, Pearl Buck (1892–1973) grew up the Chinese village of Chinkiang. She attended boarding school in Shanghai and moved to the United States in 1910 to study philosophy at Randolph-Macon Woman's College (now Randolph College). She returned to China to care for her sick mother, and moved back and forth between China and the United States throughout the 1920s. In 1930, Buck published her first novel, *East Wind: West Wind*. Her next and best-known novel, *The Good Earth*, earned her a Pulitzer Prize in 1932. In 1938 she became the first American woman to receive a Nobel Prize in literature. Throughout her life Buck was an advocate for Asian Americans, and she established several organizations to address the issues of poverty and discrimination in Asian countries.

ADOPTION

ADVOCATE

AMERICAN

ASIAN

BUCK

CAREER

CHILDREN

CHINA

CHINKIANG

DISCRIMINATION

EAST WIND: WEST WIND

THE GOOD EARTH

HUMANITARIAN

LAUREATE

LITERATURE

MISSIONARIES

NOBEL

NOVEL

ORGANIZATION

PEARL

PEASANTS

POVERTY

PRIZE

PULITZER

SHANGHAI

VILLAGE

WRITER

```
D Y T R E V O P A S I A N X T F
P I S E I R A N O I S S I M D R
E A S T W I N D W E S T W I N D
A M O C R E E R A C D C K G B T
R N S R R E P C G I W H P N E H
L A H A G I T R C S Y I E A T E
D I P S M A M I I V B L G I A G
I R T Q T E N I R Z Y D A K C O
A A R E N N R I N W E R L N O O
H T E O R O A I Z A E E L I V D
G I Z K M A I S C A T N I H D E
N N T A V B T T A A T I V C A A
A A I C V Z U U P E N I O Z N R
H M L E V O N C R O P E O N I T
S U U N O B E L K E D U H N N H
H H P H G Y L A U R E A T E C V
```

Answers on page 178.

HATTIE MCDANIEL

Hattie McDaniel (1893–1952) was the youngest of 13 children born to former slaves. She always loved to sing, and in the 1920s she became the first African American woman to sing on the radio in the U.S. She moved to Los Angeles in 1931 and landed her first film role in 1932's *The Golden West*. Throughout the 1930s, McDaniel appeared in such films as *Judge Priest, The Little Colonel, China Seas, Murder by Television,* and *Show Boat*. Her role as Mammy in 1939's *Gone with the Wind* cemented McDaniel's place as a Hollywood superstar. She won the Academy Award for Best Supporting Actress, becoming the first Black American to be nominated for and win an Oscar. She appeared in more than 300 films during her prolific career.

ACADEMY AWARD

ACTING

ACTRESS

ALICE ADAMS

BLACK

CAREER

CHINA SEAS

CLARK GABLE

DUET

FILM

FIRST

GOLDEN WEST (The)

GONE WITH THE WIND

HATTIE

HOLLYWOOD

JUDGE PRIEST

LITTLE COLONEL (The)

LOS ANGELES

MAMMY

MCDANIEL

MINSTREL

MURDER BY TELEVISION

OSCAR

PERFORM

QUEENIE

RADIO

ROLE

SARATOGA

SHIRLEY TEMPLE

SHOW BOAT

SING

STAR

VIVACIOUS LADY

WILL ROGERS

```
F I L M Y S M A D A E C I L A U Y R
O I D A R S H I R L E Y T E M P L E
N O I S I V E L E T Y B R E D R U M
L A Y V W L B P E R F O R M T T G G
E G C D V O E L G K L T M S L O J G
L N F A B I O N C H A E E A N O R N
B I I G D R V A O O O I I E M V K I
A S R O R E L A B L R L W N W M S T
G T S L K B M W C P O I L I A A Y C
K A T D A R O Y E I T C L Y E D M A
R G Q E A H E G A H O L E S W I C S
A O U N S C D E T W R U A L N O H M
L T E W K U T H R O A N S S T A O O
C A E E J S E R G A I R T L T T S D
D R N S O W T E E H C R D T A C I C
U A I T I Q R A C S E R I A A D N L
E S E N D S G R R L S E G R M P Y O
T O D P N L O S A N G E L E S M F B
```

Answers on page 178.

ELEANOR ROOSEVELT

The niece of President Theodore Roosevelt, Eleanor Roosevelt (1884–1962) was a shy and insecure child. Roosevelt lost both of her parents at a young age. At 15, Roosevelt began studying at London's Allenswood Academy. She returned to the U.S. in 1902 with newfound confidence. In 1905, she married distant cousin Franklin D. Roosevelt. When FDR took office in 1933, Roosevelt established herself as a unique first lady. She advocated for human and women's rights, gave press conferences, and wrote a newspaper column. After leaving the White House, Roosevelt became chair of the United Nations Commission on Human Rights and helped write the Universal Declaration of Human Rights. Roosevelt is remembered as one of the most widely-admired women in American history.

ADMIRED	FRANKLIN	PRESS
ALLENSWOOD	GREAT DEPRESSION	PUBLIC SERVICE
ASSEMBLY	GROUNDBREAKING	RESPECTED
CHILDREN	HUMAN RIGHTS	ROOSEVELT
CIVIL RIGHTS	HYDE PARK	SHY
COLUMN	INFLUENTIAL	THEODORE
COMMISSION	MEDIA	TRUMAN
DECLARATION	NIECE	UNITED NATIONS
DELEGATE	POLICY	WHITE HOUSE
ELEANOR	POLIO	WOMEN
EQUALITY	POLITICAL	WORLD WARS
FIRST LADY	PRESIDENT	WRITER

```
R O N A E L E C I V R E S C I L B U P
R U K E N W L M S T H G I R N A M U H
S G F X T I N F L U E N T I A L C N A
C N K I F A E Q U A L I T Y F K O Y S
I I G N R H G C H I L D R E N I C N P
V K R O U S D E I P R E S S S I O H W
I A E I R M T E L B E X G S L I Y O R
L E A T L E N L R E Q I I O T D R E T
R R T A N D T S A I D M P A E L S L A
I B D R O I B I J D M J N P D P E S N
G D E A I A E D R O Y D A W E V S I T
H N P L L Y A C C W E R A C E E L E N
T U R C O H C M E T K R T S M K I R E
S O E E P S Y O I B S E O B N T R O D
E R S D T S K N L E D O L A W R W D I
F G S Z T J U Z G U R Y R F Y U O O S
W H I T E H O U S E M F G D F M M E E
Q P O L I T I C A L W N S Z R A E H R
N X N Y K D O O W S N E L L A N N T P
```

Answers on page 179.

MARGARET CHASE SMITH

Margaret Chase Smith (1897–1995) was the first woman to serve in both chambers of Congress and the first woman to represent Maine in either. When her husband, Clyde, was elected to the House of Representatives in 1936, Smith worked as his secretary. After he died in 1940, Smith ran for his seat and won. Following eight years in the House, Smith successfully ran for Senate. A moderate Republican, she was an early critic of McCarthyism. In her famous 1950 "Declaration of Conscience" speech, Smith denounced "hate and character assassination," though failed to mention fellow Republican Joseph McCarthy by name. She was a skilled diplomat and legislator, traveling the world and meeting the leaders of 23 different nations. Smith received more than 90 honorary degrees and the Presidential Medal of Freedom in 1989.

ACTIVITIES	HOUSE	REPUBLICAN
CLYDE	LEGISLATOR	SEAT
COMMITTEE	MAINE	SECRETARY
COMMUNISM	MCCARTHYISM	SENATE
CONGRESS	MEDAL	SERVICE
CONSCIENCE	MILITARY	SPEECH
DECLARATION	MODERATE	TENURE
DIPLOMAT	NAVY	UN-AMERICAN
ELECTED	NEW DEAL	WOMAN
FIRST	POLITICS	
FREEDOM	REPRESENTATIVE	

```
H C E E P S M W N E T T D A J C
N Y V A N P O S C E A A C G H L
M K I D K M O I I M W T E R O Y
I F T D A D V L O N I D O S U D
L E A N M R S L I V U T E Q S E
I E T C E S P E I T A M D A E U
T T N S O I I T C L I E M Q L N
A T E E D N I Y S R C C C O E A
R I S T T E S I H L E O S M C M
Y M E A S A G C A T N T O M T E
E M R N T E R R I G R D A M E R
N O P E L S A E R E E A E R D I
I C E S U T R E D E N D C L Y C
A O R E I W S I R O A C J C V A
M Q Y O J S M F F L M E E D M N
T E N U R E R E P U B L I C A N
```

Answers on page 179.

LUCILLE BALL

Before Cher, Madonna, and Beyoncé made the single-name moniker popular, there was Lucille Ball (1911–1989)–known to millions around the world as simply "Lucy." In 1926, Ball enrolled in a New York City drama school, though her teachers thought she lacked talent. Throughout the 1930s, she landed small parts in films and on Broadway. During this time, Ball worked with comic legends like the Three Stooges, the Marx Brothers, Laurel and Hardy, and Buster Keaton, learning lessons that would shape the rest of her career. Ball met and married Cuban bandleader Desi Arnaz in 1940. In 1951, she and Desi created the sitcom *I Love Lucy*, which ultimately ran for six seasons and won five Emmy Awards. The couple's production company, Desilu, went on to produce hit shows including *Star Trek* and *Mission: Impossible*.

ACTRESS	CBS	FILM	PRODUCTION
AUDIENCE	COMIC	HOUSEWIFE	RATINGS
AWARDS	COMPANY	I LOVE LUCY	SHOW
B MOVIES	COUPLE	MARRIAGE	SITCOM
BALL	DESI ARNAZ	NEW YORK	SPIN-OFF
BROADWAY	DESILU	PILOT	STUDIO
BUSINESS	DRAMA	PIONEER	TELEVISION
CAREER	EMMY	PRODUCER	TOUR

```
M K P E Y D V I X M O C T I S F
D Q C G M C E B R O A D W A Y G
E C A A L A U S W S E I V O M B
S O R I I C U L I J Y E S P W C
I U E R F B B D E A E M I T D O
L P E R E S Z F I V R L M H T M
U L R A T I N G S E O N A E E I
A E N M A M A R D T N L A K L C
Y F N C S P I N O F F C I Z E C
S I K R O Y W E N J V W E N V O
S W P R O D U C T I O N X I I M
E E O O H H B U S I N E S S S P
R S R E E N O I P R U O T P I A
T U W O H S A A W A R D S G O N
C O X F R E C U D O R P N H N Y
A H G Q L S T U D I O L L A B B
```

Answers on page 179.

RACHEL CARSON

Rachel Carson (1907–1964) grew up with the twin loves of nature and writing. She studied biology at Pennsylvania College for Women (now Chatham University), then zoology at Johns Hopkins University. In 1935, Carson went to work for the U.S. Bureau of Fisheries, where she wrote educational copy that explored aquatic life. Carson wrote a trilogy of books about the ocean–1941's *Under the Sea Wind*, 1951's *The Sea Around Us*, and 1955's *The Edge of the Sea*–that described sea life in clear, non-technical prose. *The Sea Around Us* was serialized in the *New Yorker*, won a National Book Award, and spent 86 weeks on the *New York Times* Best Seller list. Carson's 1962 book *Silent Spring*, which outlined the dangers of chemical pesticides like DDT, helped spark the environmental movement.

AQUATIC

AUTHOR

AWARD

BEST-SELLER

BIOLOGY

BOOK

BUREAU

CARSON

CHEMICAL

CONSERVATION

DDT

DOROTHY FREEMAN

EDGE OF THE SEA (The)

ENVIRONMENT

FISHERIES

LETTERS

MAINE

MARINE

NATURE

NIECE

OCEAN

PESTICIDES

RACHEL

SEA AROUND US (The)

SILENT SPRING

UNDER THE SEA WIND

WRITER

ZOOLOGY

```
T S V C O N S E R V A T I O N P T O
Y E H D R B Y A N F S N U W A S R S
W D E N E J O A X Y T A M F M E T I
N I D I R N T O Z J E O F I E A L L
O C G W W U I U K R R C M S E A O E
S I E A R T V R U Z E I B H R R A N
R T O E L N L B A A T H I E F O D T
A S F S L E C A H M I L O R Y U Z S
C E T E E M T I C I R H L I H N U P
R P H H U N Z T T I W A O E T D E R
M A E T B O T C E A M L G S O U H I
Z S S R T R T A L R U E Y H R S N N
O E E E U I O V Q A S Q H G O D I G
O N A D K V C C W E V S A C D D E X
L I J N B N S A E R O H T U A T C W
O A E U Y E R Q V A Q D X C P E E X
G M Y V J D H B Q M N U L E H C A R
Y V M B E S T S E L L E R E N P Q K
```

Answers on page 179.

ELLA FITZGERALD

Known as the "First Lady of Song" and "Queen of Jazz," Ella Fitzgerald (1917–1996) was a popular vocalist who interpreted much of the Great American Songbook. As a girl, Fitzgerald fell in love with Louis Armstrong, Bing Crosby, and the Boswell Sisters. In 1934, Fitzgerald won an amateur singing contest at Harlem's Apollo Theater, launching her career. Fitzgerald joined the Chick Webb Orchestra, and worked with other groups as well. Her first major hit, "A-Tisket, A-Tasket," made Fitzgerald a household name. In the 1940s, she toured with Dizzy Gillespie and started incorporating scat singing into her performances. In the 1950s and '60s, she recorded nearly 250 songs by composers such as George Gershwin and Cole Porter. Fitzgerald was the first African American woman to win a Grammy Award, and won 14 Grammys in her lifetime.

APOLLO	FIRST LADY OF SONG	QUEEN OF JAZZ
AWARD	FITZGERALD	RANGE
BALLROOM	GERSHWIN (George)	RECORDING
BEBOP	GRAMMY	SCAT
BENNY GOODMAN	HARLEM	SINGER
CHICK WEBB	INTERPRET	SONGBOOK
CONTEST	NORMAN GRANZ	STYLE
DECCA	ORCHESTRA	VERVE
DIZZY GILLESPIE	PHILHARMONIC	VIRGINIA
ELLA	POPULAR	VOICE
	PORTER (Cole)	

```
A G Y M M A R G T S E T N O C G F S
S N W C N Q S C A T M Z X A B U I O
R I T D I S S K V S P O R T E R T N
R W Z I M N I T Z T T D O T U N Z G
N H Z Z E V O N Y D I R O R G O G B
O S A Z V G O M G L X A H N L K E O
R R J Y R E N I E E W R A C L R O
M E F G E R H I C A R A A O B D A K
A G O I V A G S D E H R L B E P L B
N H N L R O X B D R T L E R O L D Z
G W E L P O B E B S O W I P V E L C
R W E E R D N V E P K C U H C O M A
A M U S A X M H A C H L E C P D K B
N T Q P Y M C G I Y A V A R J P W X
Z C K I P R E H W R V I R G I N I A
S G E E O Y C V B I N T E R P R E T
B E N N Y G O O D M A N E G N A R S
U Z A F I R S T L A D Y O F S O N G
```

Answers on page 180.

GRACE HOPPER

Grace Hopper (1906–1992) showed an early interest in mathematics and physics, which she studied at Vassar College. She went on to earn a PhD in mathematics from Yale University in 1934. Hopper taught math at Vassar until World War II broke out. She joined the U.S. Navy and was assigned to program the Mark I computer. Hopper continued to work in computing after the war. She moved to private industry in 1949, first with the Eckert-Mauchly Computer Corporation, then with Remington Rand, where she oversaw development of UNIVAC, the first all-electronic digital computer. In 1952, Hopper's team created the first computer compiler, a program that translates written instructions into codes that computers can read. Hopper resumed active naval service at the age of 60, becoming a rear admiral before retiring in 1986.

ADMIRAL	ECKERT-MAUCHLY	MILITARY	TEAM
AMAZING		NAVY	TRANSLATE
BUG	GRACE	PHYSICS	UNIVAC
CODE	HOPPER	PROFESSOR	VASSAR
COMPILER	INDUSTRY	PROGRAM	WOMAN
COMPUTER	LANGUAGE	RAND	YALE
CORPORATION	LEADER	RANK	
DEVELOP	MARK I	REMINGTON	
DIGITAL	MATH	SOFTWARE	

```
H O P P E R E G E C A R G X A Y
E R A W T F O S E Y W I I R E A
Y W E E I W G G F V P P T E D L
L C J L O K A C T A R R N D O E
H T A M I U R L E N O O D A C I
C K A V G P A A E S F G E E P N
U N N N I T M H M Z E R V L H D
A N A A I N G O Q A S A E M Y U
M L A G R G U U C D S M L I S S
T Y I M R E T U P M O C O L I T
R D F V A S S A R I R D P I C R
E R B E S Z C V I R N P T T S Y
K U R G R Y I T R A N S L A T E
C W U T E A M N R L F R U R R P
E B R R E M I N G T O N O Y M K
C W O H C O R P O R A T I O N Q
```

Answers on page 180.

ROSA PARKS

Rosa Parks (1913–2005) was actively involved in the Civil Rights Movement in Alabama. She joined the Montgomery chapter of the National Association for the Advancement of Colored People (NAACP) in 1943 and served as youth leader and secretary to President E.D. Nixon until 1957. Her defining moment occurred on December 1, 1955. After a long day's work as a seamstress at a Montgomery department store, Parks refused to surrender her seat to a White passenger on a segregated bus. Parks was arrested, found guilty of violating a local ordinance, and fined $10. Her defiance sparked the Montgomery Bus Boycott and inspired other efforts to end racial segregation. On November 13, 1956, the Supreme Court ruled that racial segregation on public transit was unconstitutional, and the boycott officially ended on December 20 of that year.

ACTIVIST	FINED	RESISTANCE
ALABAMA	GUILTY	RIDE
ARRESTED	LAWYER	SEAMSTRESS
BOYCOTT	LEADER	SEAT
BUS	MONTGOMERY	SECRETARY
CIVIL RIGHTS	MOVEMENT	SEGREGATION
COURAGE	NAACP	STORE
DEFIANCE	ORDINANCE	SUPREME COURT
DEPARTMENT	PASSENGER	YOUTH

```
R E M T Z X C H E B S R D I S S
I D N A A C P Q U K T C N S E R
D L E D T K D S N S O O O U A L
E M C T E M H E I R R U I P M K
S L N A S F O V N K E R T R S T
E E A M A E I N O I G A A E T N
C A N A S T R A T M F G G M R E
R D I B C E H R N G I E E E E M
E E D A H D A T A C O B R C S T
T R R L V E E T U G E M G O S R
A O O A T T O C Y O B K E U H A
R V L A W Y E R G U Y F S R M P
Y O A J T N E M E V O M W T Y E
A C I V I L R I G H T S C Y C D
U G O Z R E G N E S S A P M U I
Y T L I U G R E S I S T A N C E
```

Answers on page 180.

KATHERINE JOHNSON

Katherine Johnson (1918–2020) was an exceptionally bright child who started high school at age 10. She then enrolled in West Virginia State College, and at 18 graduated summa cum laude with degrees in mathematics and French. In 1952, Johnson learned that the National Advisory Committee for Aeronautics (NACA) was hiring African American women to serve as "computers." She accepted a position there the following year. In the late 1950s, after NACA became the National Aeronautics and Space Administration (NASA), Johnson tackled her most notable work–plotting the path of space flights. Her accurate and precise calculations proved crucial for Alan Shepard's first flight to space, John Glenn's orbit around Earth, and the Apollo missions to the moon. In 2015, Johnson was awarded the Presidential Medal of Freedom. Her story was depicted in the 2016 film *Hidden Figures*.

ACCURATE	EARTH	LAUNCH	PRECISE
AFRICAN AMERICAN	FLIGHT	MATHEMATICS	RESEARCH
	FRENCH	MEDAL	RETURN
APOLLO	HIDDEN FIGURES	MISSION	SPACE
ASTRONAUTS		MOON	TRAILBLAZER
BRILLIANT	INSPIRING	NACA	TRAJECTORY
BUILDING	JOHNSON	NASA	WEST VIRGINIA
CALCULATIONS	KATHERINE	PATH	
COMPUTER	LANGLEY	PIONEER	WOMAN

```
Z M A I N I G R I V T S E W F F K L
E A P Y T Q D R X H D T J H N H X F
N T I N N E J R G Q S M I G R C A U
I H O A A A Y I L T K D S U U N F E
R E N M I R L R U D D E O I T E R I
E M E O L F E A O E A S A N E R I N
H A E W L J N Z N T H B F R R F C S
T T R E I O O F A C C U R A T E A P
A I S A R G I H R L A E W P V H N I
K C P T B G N A N L B P J N I Q A R
C S S R U K E I A S V L O A C H M I
O A G R E S M N D F O I I L R A E N
M H E V E C G E P L S N A A L T R G
P S M R X L I A D S I O B C R O I N
U N I X E G T S I A M U H G A T C S
T O G Y O H J M E P L J B F W N A V
E O O M E C A P S S L A U N C H N Y
R M M E V C C A L C U L A T I O N S
```

Answers on page 180.

RUBY BRIDGES

Ruby Bridges (1954–) and her family moved to New Orleans in 1958. Although the landmark case of *Brown v. Board of Education* was decided in 1954, schools in the South had been slow to integrate. The school board of New Orleans' William Frantz Elementary decided to require an entrance exam for prospective Black students, hoping the school would stay all-White. But Bridges passed the exam, and on November 14, 1960, she walked into the school, accompanied by her mother and four federal marshals. White parents pulled their children out of classes, and all but one teacher, Barbara Henry, refused to teach Bridges. In 1999, Bridges founded the Ruby Bridges Foundation to uphold "values of tolerance, respect, and appreciation of all differences." President Bill Clinton awarded Bridges the Presidential Citizens Medal in 2001.

ALL-WHITE	FEDERAL	ROCKWELL
BOARD	FOUNDATION	RUBY
BRIDGES	HENRY	SCHOOL
BROWN	INTEGRATE	SEGREGATION
CIVIL RIGHTS	MARSHALS	SIX
CLASS	MEDAL	SOUTH
DISCRIMINATION	NEW ORLEANS	STUDENTS
EDUCATION	PAINTING	TEACHER
ELEMENTARY	PARENTS	TOLERANCE
ENTRANCE	RACISM	WILLIAM FRANTZ
EXAM	RESPECT	

```
O Y R N E H N O I T A C U D E U Q P
M M H T E C N A R T N E A Y A K L N
B A S J B S I N T E G R A T E A O J
R N R S T E A C H E R N W E Z I B E
I C O S T H G I R L I V I C T S I X
D L J I H R O C K W E L L A N O T F
G A M S T A C M G N L E N R A N O Y
E S L C C A L O K V X I I A R H L R
S S H F P H G S C A M D S C F A E A
S E U O G V O E M I Y R T I M L R T
K T U U N E W O R L E A N S A L A N
T D U N V B C L G G O E M I W N E
C T O D J L S R S K E B R Y L H C M
E Q Y A E I A O O V H S A E L I E E
P B B T D N U D J W U Q P G I T N L
S U U I T T T F E K N H X U W E F E
E M R O H S W S A M F L A R E D E F
R P S N T G N I T N I A P T P S A A
```

Answers on page 181.

HARPER LEE

Harper Lee (1926–2016) is best known for writing the 1960 novel *To Kill a Mockingbird*, which contains details from her own childhood. Born in racially divided Monroeville, Alabama, Lee was a tomboy, just like the book's protagonist, Scout Finch, with an attorney father. After briefly attending law school, Lee moved to New York City in 1949 to pursue a writing career. She struggled to support herself. In 1956, Lee's friend, Broadway composer Michael Martin Brown, offered to support her for a year so she could write full time. Lee wrote what became *To Kill a Mockingbird*. The Pulitzer Prize-winning best seller has been translated into 40 languages and sells more than a million copies a year. She assisted childhood friend Truman Capote with his book *In Cold Blood*. In 2015, Lee released *Go Set a Watchman*, which follows the later years of the Finch family.

ALABAMA	FICTION	NOVEL
ATTICUS	FINCH	PRIZE
BEST SELLER	HARPER	PULITZER
BOO RADLEY	IN COLD BLOOD	SCOUT
BOOK	JEM	TOMBOY
BROWN	LEE	TRIAL
CAPOTE	MOCKINGBIRD	WATCHMAN
DILL	NELLIE	WRITING
FAMILY	NEW YORK CITY	

```
H P Y L N E W Y O R K C I T Y A
L A L R E G E C E S H H K U B H
X J I G E E R Z D L A T U O F O
M X M U E L T R L R U F E C R S
O E A M V I L I P T Z Y S S L U
C N F W L W D E Q T H C N I F C
K U O U W T R J S R W A B R Z I
I C P V P R I N R T M F K S E T
N A Z A E B I E O H S A M Z J T
G P I D O L I T C I M E I P E A
B O L O L L O T I A T R B L M S
I T K X L M A F B N P C P A I I
R E L E B W H A C F G J I S B I
D K N O Y E L D A R O O B F M B
L C Y X Z A B R O W N T R I A L
E F W C H I N C O L D B L O O D
```

Answers on page 181.

DOLORES HUERTA

Activist and labor leader Dolores Huerta (1930–) was raised in Stockton, California. After becoming a teacher and seeing the poor living conditions of many of her students, Huerta helped form the Community Services Organization, which led voter registration drives and worked to improve social and economic conditions for Hispanics. In 1960, she created the Agricultural Workers Association. In 1962, Huerta and Cesar Chavez founded the National Farm Workers Association, which later became the United Farm Workers' Union (UFW). Huerta served as UFW vice president until 1999, organizing workers, leading strikes and boycotts, negotiating contracts, and advocating for safer working conditions, including eliminating harmful pesticides. Huerta won several awards for her advocacy for workers' and immigrants' rights, including the Eleanor Roosevelt Award for Human Rights and the Presidential Medal of Freedom.

ACTIVIST	DOLORES	NEGOTIATOR
AGRICULTURE	FARM	ORGANIZER
ASSOCIATION	FERNÁNDEZ	PESTICIDES
AWARD	GRAPE BOYCOTTS	SERVICES
CHAVEZ	HISPANIC	STOCKTON
CHICANO	HUERTA	UFW
COMMUNITY	LABOR	UNION
CONDITIONS	LEADER	VICE PRESIDENT
CONTRACTS	MEXICAN AMERICAN	WAGES
DELANO STRIKE		WORKERS

```
G R A P E B O Y C O T T S P N V
R O O E K I R T S O N A L E D K
O B R A H O G K L E A D E R I T
N A G S E G A W S T O C K T O N
A L A S Z E D N A N R E F I F E
C C N O A P P S R E K R O W A D
I O I C W N E G O T I A T O R I
H N Z I A M B S E R O L O D M S
C T E A R U F W T C H A V E Z E
U R R T D L S E C I V R E S Z R
N A C I R E M A N A C I X E M P
I C U O J V A C T I V I S T T E
O T K N H I S P A N I C D F T C
N S A A G R I C U L T U R E R I
Y Z A M C O M M U N I T Y P S V
S N O I T I D N O C H U E R T A
```

Answers on page 181.

BETTY FRIEDAN

Betty Friedan (1921–2006) lost her job as a reporter after becoming pregnant with her second child. Friedan stayed home to raise her children, even though she felt unfulfilled in this role. Wondering if other women felt the same, Friedan surveyed college graduates and discovered that many housewives felt depressed and dissatisfied with their lives. She used her findings to write her 1963 book, *The Feminine Mystique,* a best seller often credited with spurring "second wave" feminism in the United States. Friedan went on to cofound the National Organization for Women in 1966. As its first president, Friedan lobbied for equal pay for women and to outlaw discrimination in the workplace. She helped found the National Association for the Repeal of Abortion Laws (now known as NARAL Pro-Choice America) in 1969, and with other leading feminists helped create the National Women's Political Caucus in 1971.

BERKELEY

BEST SELLER

BETTY

BEYOND GENDER

BOOK

CHILDREN

EQUAL PAY

FEMININE MYSTIQUE (The)

FEMINIST

FOUNTAIN OF AGE (The)

FRIEDAN

GENDER ROLES

HOUSEWIFE

LIFE SO FAR

MOVEMENT

NARAL

ORGANIZATION

POLITICAL CAUCUS

PRESIDENT

PSYCHOLOGY

REPORTER

RIGHTS

SECOND STAGE (The)

SECOND WAVE

SMITH COLLEGE

SURVEY

WOMEN

WORKPLACE

WRITER

```
Y P S C N T N E R D L I H C F L Y K
U S U B E Y O N D G E N D E R T R E
S Y C D N B V Y Y Y N Y L B E X E X
M C U P R Z E Z E E A B E C O U X R
I H A H U T V S M F T P A V Q O T E
T O C R E N O O T O I L L I R F K G
H L L A G E W R F S P W T A O U F A
C O A F B M S C G K E S E U U E S T
O G C O W E S E R A Y L N S M Q T S
L Y I S R V R O L M N T L I U N E D
L R T E I O W K E O A I N E E O I N
E I I F T M N N E I R I Z D R B H O
G G L I E A I M N L S R I A E B O C
E H O L R N A O K T E S E T T F M E
L T P A I L F K T W E Y T D B I V S
M S L M N A D E I R F Y P S N P O G
S T E R G T Y M P R E T R O P E R N
T F U E V A W D N O C E S L M W G X
```

Answers on page 181.

PATSY MINK

Patsy Mink (1927–2002) grew up in Hawaii and experienced discrimination throughout her life. After earning degrees in zoology and chemistry at the University of Hawaii, Mink received her Juris Doctor degree from the University of Chicago Law School. Mink passed the Hawaii bar exam in 1953, but was unable to find a job because of her interracial marriage (her husband was White). She started her own practice and became the first Japanese American woman to practice law in Hawaiian territory. When Hawaii became a state in 1959, Mink took an interest in politics and served in the Hawaii State Senate. In 1964, Mink won a seat in the U.S. House of Representatives, making her the first Asian American woman elected to Congress. Mink focused on equal rights for all and helped author Title IX, which required public schools to provide gender-equitable treatment in education and athletics.

ASIAN AMERICAN	FIRST	SEAT
ATHLETICS	GENDER EQUITABLE	SIX TERMS
AUTHOR	HAWAII	STATE SENATE
BAR EXAM	HOUSE	TERRITORY
CHEMISTRY	JAPANESE AMERICAN	TITLE IX
CONGRESS	LAWYER	TREATMENT
DEMOCRAT	MINK	UNIVERSITY
DISCRIMINATION	PATSY	WOMAN
EDUCATION	POLITICS	WON
ELECTED	PRACTICE	ZOOLOGY
EQUAL RIGHTS	REPRESENTATIVES	

```
C V E E S U O H Y R T S I M E H C P
N A C I R E M A E S E N A P A J F L
N M U L E L E C T E D P N A M O W E
O N A T N E M T A E R T A B I P D L
W O A X C O N G R E S S F T Y J L B
G I T S E R S H H S E A T I S U S A
E T P E I R M I N K C L O C R Y T T
Q A R Y Y A A C U I L Z I Z T S A I
U N A T G U N B T A I T B I A K T U
A I C I R O E A W E E A T B R Q E Q
L M T S O I L Y M L R L W U G D S E
R I I R H I E O H E E R Q A F E E R
I R C E T R A T O I R L I T H M N E
G C E V U Y A F X Z A I Y T X O A D
H S S I A M P O L I T I C S O C T N
T I C N O I T A C U D E U A F R E E
S D J U Q L S M R E T X I S N A Y G
S E V I T A T N E S E R P E R T U L
```

Answers on page 182.

LADY BIRD JOHNSON

Claudia "Lady Bird" Johnson (1912–2007) grew up in a wealthy Texas family and was considered especially well-educated for a woman of her era. She married Lyndon B. Johnson in 1934 and helped fund his congressional campaign and run his office after he was elected. When Lyndon Johnson became vice president to John F. Kennedy, Lady Bird often served as Jaqueline Kennedy's substitute at official events. When Kennedy was assassinated and LBJ became president, Lady Bird led a national effort to beautify the country and the capital. As first lady, she supported the Highway Beautification Act, promoted the Civil Rights Act, and served as an advisor to her husband. With Lady Bird's support, more than 100 laws on the environment passed during Johnson's presidency. She received the Presidential Medal of Freedom and the Congressional Gold Medal.

ACT	ENVIRONMENT	LBJ
ADVISOR	FAMILY	LIBRARY
AUSTIN	FIRST LADY	MEDAL
BEAUTIFICATION	FLOWERS	PARKS
CAMPAIGN	GREAT SOCIETY	PRESIDENCY
CAPITAL	HEAD START	PROJECT
CIVIL RIGHTS	HIGHWAY	SUPPORT
CLAUDIA	JOHNSON	TEXAS
CONGRESS	KENNEDY	TOUR
COUNTRY	LADY BIRD	WAR ON POVERTY
DIARY	LAWS	WHITE HOUSE

```
J J V Y T E I C O S T A E R G F B
F C O U N T R Y F I R S T L A D Y
N Y T W D J Y D B V L H C M Q E R
O T N U R T R E E T B G I Q S O K
S R E T I C A N A E J L Z U S L T
N E M S B A I N U X Y Y O I T A R
H V N R Y C D E T A S H V O N D A
O O O E D F A K I S E D U A N E T
J P R W A X I P F T A R Q X I M S
S N I O L C I V I L R I G H T S D
S O V L E I F H C T P A R K S T A
E R N F M J W A A N A G M E U V E
R A E D I J S F T M U L U W A V H
G W L Y R A R B I L A I D U A L C
N G I A P M A C O H I G H W A Y I
O T C E J O R P N G S U P P O R T
C C P R E S I D E N C Y T S W A L
```

Answers on page 182.

FANNIE LOU HAMER

Fannie Lou Hamer (1917–1977) was the youngest of 20 children born to sharecroppers. She married in 1944 and wanted to start a family of her own. However, a White doctor gave Hamer a hysterectomy without her consent during surgery to remove a tumor. In 1962, Hamer attended a Student Nonviolent Coordinating Committee (SNCC) meeting encouraging African Americans to register to vote. When Hamer's boss discovered she'd tried to register, he fired her. Hamer dedicated the rest of her life to fighting for civil rights. In 1964, Hamer cofounded the Mississippi Freedom Democratic Party, which opposed her state's all-White delegation to that year's Democratic National Convention. She called for mandatory integrated state delegations in a televised speech at the convention. Hamer cofounded the National Women's Political Caucus in 1971. She was inducted into the National Women's Hall of Fame in 1993.

CAUCUS	HAMER	REGISTER
CIVIL RIGHTS	HYSTERECTOMY	SCHOOL
COFOUNDER	INTEGRATION	SHARECROPPER
COMMITTEE	LEADER	SNCC
CONVENTION	LOU	SOUTH
DELEGATION	MANDATORY	SPEECH
DEMOCRATIC	MISSISSIPPI	STUDENT
FANNIE	NATIONAL	TELEVISED
FREEDOM	NONVIOLENT	VOTE
GROUP	PARTY	WOMEN'S
HALL OF FAME	POLITICAL	WORK

```
Z W D Y M O T C E R E T S Y H S R
I S W N A T I O N A L O D D R H E
J N T U G R O U P S V E E E S A D
I C T H Y R O T A D N A M S T R A
P I C E G I B D U U O C L I U E E
P T O R G I S P E E C H C V D C L
I A N Z E R R H P L M O D E E R F
S R V U J I A L A A E F O L N O L
S C E H O R N T I L R G C E T P O
I O N T S L E N I V L T A T P P O
S M T U U S G G A O I O Y T G E H
S E I O C Y N A I F N C F O I R C
I D O S U U B E D S Q N D F R O S
M C N L A C O M M I T T E E A V N
L C L A C I T I L O P E M W O M O
R R E D N U O F O C W A R T U C E
N O N V I O L E N T H H E W O R K
```

Answers on page 182.

RITA MORENO

Born in Puerto Rico, Rita Moreno (1931–) moved to New York City in 1936, where she began taking dancing lessons. She made her Broadway debut and landed her first film role in her early teens. Moreno is best-known for playing Anita in *West Side Story*, for which she became the first Hispanic actress to win an Academy Award. In 1971, she joined the cast of the children's program *The Electric Company*, earning a Grammy for the soundtrack. Moreno won a Tony for her part in *The Ritz*. Guest appearances on *The Muppet Show* and *The Rockford Files* earned her Emmys, making Moreno the first Latina and the third person in history to achieve an EGOT after winning all four major entertainment awards: an Emmy (1977, 1978), Grammy (1972), Oscar (1962), and Tony (1975). Moreno has received numerous other honors, and continues to act, sing, and perform.

ACTRESS

ANITA

ARTS

AWARDS

BROADWAY

CARNAL KNOWLEDGE

EGOT

ELECTRIC COMPANY (The)

EMMY

ENTERTAINMENT

GRAMMY

HEY, YOU GUYS!

HONORS

LATINA

MARLOWE

MEDAL

MUPPET SHOW (The)

ONE DAY AT A TIME

OSCAR

OZ

PEABODY

PERFORMANCE

POPI

PROGRAM

PUERTO RICO

RITA MORENO

RITZ (The)

ROCKFORD FILES (The)

SERIES

SINGER

SUMMER AND SMOKE

TONY

WEST SIDE STORY

```
Y E Y W E P O P I W O H S T E P P U M
G R R E N T E R T A I N M E N T E A E
R H O H O N O R S Y V O T W U M N G X
A E T O Y J J U A N A S O G M E D K O
M C S L N A N B I A J C G Y Y E P U N
M B E A L A W A R D S A E D L E H M E
Y B D D Z Y N O T O S R O W R E K A R
R R I E S T Y U C M Q B O F Y N A R O
C O S M Z N I I K Y A N O Y R R B G M
S A T S E C R R S E K R O R T N L O A
I D S Q E O H G P L M U L S R Z A R T
N W E B T R S X A A G I A O F K T P I
G A W R Y E T N N U C J N V W I I B R
E Y E O R R R C Y A T I N A R E N O E
R U J I Y A E S A L C S Z E A R A R Z
P G E D C S U M M E R A N D S M O K E
D S M Y N A P M O C C I R T C E L E X
L V Q S E L I F D R O F K C O R T T E
B M V F O N E D A Y A T A T I M E F G
```

Answers on page 182.

SHIRLEY CHISHOLM

After working in education early in her career, Shirley Chisholm (1924–2005) began taking an interest in politics in the 1960s, and in 1965 became a member of the New York State Assembly. In 1968, she was elected to the U.S. House of Representatives, becoming the first Black congresswoman. In 1972, Chisholm made history again when she announced a bid for the U.S. presidency, becoming the first woman to run for the Democratic Party's nomination. Although Chisholm lost the nomination, she went on to serve seven terms in the House as an outspoken advocate for women and minorities before returning to teaching. She taught politics and sociology at Mount Holyoke College until 1987. Chisholm was posthumously awarded the Presidential Medal of Freedom in 2015.

ADVOCATE	FIRST	REPRESENTATIVES
AUTHOR	FREEDOM	SERVE
BID	HISTORY	SEVEN TERMS
BLACK	HOUSE	SHIRLEY
BROOKLYN	LEADERSHIP	SOCIOLOGY
CAMPAIGN	MEDAL	STATE ASSEMBLY
CHISHOLM	MOUNT HOLYOKE	TEACHER
CONGRESSWOMAN	NEW YORK	UNBOSSED
DISTRICT	NOMINATION	UNBOUGHT
EDUCATION	POLITICS	
ELECTED	PRESIDENCY	

```
T H G U O B N U Y Y E S U O H S S
N I R B P R E S I D E N C Y T E D
Q A B N D D T Z U M N L M Q V J A
A Y M F O E I C N G O V R I E D T
U L G O A M A S I Y D D T I S U P
T B T C W T I A T E L A E E H O C
H M H A I S P N T R T K V E L S P
O E Y O D M S C A N I E O I R I V
R S N G A V E E T N C T O H F D
C S H C O L O S R T I I T S R K E
H A T I E L E C E G C O R K R B S
I E F A S R O R A S N E N O K L S
S T E I P T M I Q T D O Y V C A O
H A V E R S O D C A E W C F A D B
O T R G O S I R E O E X D J L E N
L S E G W B T L Y N S K N O B M U
M O S C E K O Y L O H T N U O M W
```

Answers on page 183.

CAROL BURNETT

After high school, Carol Burnett (1933–) attended UCLA, with the intention of majoring in journalism. But halfway through her first year, she decided to switch her major to theater. The shy, insecure student was a natural on stage, coaxing laughter from the audience with her cut-up antics. Burnett's big break came from a Tony-nominated stint on Broadway starring in the musical comedy *Once Upon a Mattress*. An Emmy-winning run on the CBS variety program *The Garry Moore Show* followed, cementing Burnett's place in the comedy world. In 1967 *The Carol Burnett Show* debuted. The program—the first of its kind hosted by a woman—was a huge hit throughout its 11-season run. In 2013, Burnett received the Mark Twain Prize for American Humor at the Kennedy Center Honors.

AWARDS	HONORS	PRIMETIME
BROADWAY	HOST	PROGRAM
BURNETT (Carol)	HUMOR	SEASONS
CALAMITY JANE	KENNEDY CENTER	SKETCHES
CBS	KORMAN (Harvey)	SPECIALS
COMEDIAN	LAUGH	STAGE
DEBUT	LAWRENCE (Vicki)	THEATER
EMMY	MARK TWAIN PRIZE	TONY
FUNNY		UCLA
	MUSICAL	
GARRY MOORE SHOW (The)		VARIETY
	ONCE UPON A MATTRESS	WAGGONER (Lyle)
GOLDEN GLOBE		
	ONE MORE TIME	

W J O Y J R N A M R O K N B N O U
A B U R N E T T R E T A E H T N L
G P Q S J M L H B R I S Y C R C A
G V N H N A U R F D V P T A E E W
O O Y T U O O S E T S E U L T U R
N U L G R A S M I R L C B A N P E
E C H D D O O A O C O I E M E O N
R L T W E C M N E N A A D I C N C
V A A H E N O U E S T L E T Y A E
A Y S U M H G M H E S S G Y D M P
S D R A W A O L L E O E A J E A R
R Y T E I R A V O L H A T A N T O
E M I T E M I R P B C Y S N N T G
S K E T C H E S X Z E B M E E R R
C G I T O N Y Y N N U F S M K E A
A M A R K T W A I N P R I Z E S M
E G A R R Y M O O R E S H O W S C

Answers on page 183.

GLORIA STEINEM

After studying government at Smith College, Gloria Steinem (1934–) began a career as a freelance writer. One of her first and most famous articles was an exposé of New York City's Playboy Club for *Show* magazine. Steinem went undercover as a Playboy "bunny" to research her article, which exposed the sexism and exploitation the women at the club endured. In 1968, Steinem helped found *New York* magazine, where she became an editor and writer covering political campaigns and progressive social issues, including the women's liberation movement. Her insert for the magazine eventually became the feminist magazine, *Ms.* In 1971, Steinem joined other prominent feminists in founding the National Women's Political Caucus, which recruits, trains, and supports pro-choice women candidates for elected office. Steinem remains active in feminist and social issues, and has won numerous awards and honors throughout her career.

ARTICLE	GLORIA	POLITICAL
BOOKS	GOVERNMENT	PRO-CHOICE
BUNNY	JOURNALIST	PROGRESSIVE
CAUCUS	LECTURER	SEXISM
CENTER	LIBERATION	SHOW
EDITOR	MAGAZINE	SOCIAL ISSUES
EQUALITY	MEDIA	STEINEM
EXPOSÉ	MOVEMENT	WOMEN
FEMINIST	NEW YORK	WRITER
FOUNDER	ORGANIZATION	
GENDER	PLAYBOY CLUB	

```
Z S E R K G O V E R N M E N T B V
G J V N E O R G A N I Z A T I O N
G O I A I D E M C M O V E M E N T
W U S V B Z N L A C I T I L O P D
O R S M O M A E X P O S E W O H S
M N E Y O U E G G A R T I C L E R
E A R Z K R R N A W E T Z R F B E
N L G O S L B E I M T P P E E U T
R I O Y T W I U R E R M F T M L N
E S R I Y I D B N U T K N I I C E
D T P O W Q D V E N T S W R N Y C
N I R Z S Z L E Z R Y C S W I O M
U Y T I L A U Q E R A U E M S B S
O A I R O L G J G B C T A L T Y I
F N E W Y O R K S U G Q I U L A X
J S E U S S I L A I C O S O I L E
P R O C H O I C E R C S L Y N P S
```

Answers on page 183.

MAYA ANGELOU

When Maya Angelou (1928–2014) was only seven years old, she was raped by her mother's boyfriend. The experience so traumatized Angelou that she stopped speaking for five years. She found solace in literature. Her singing and acting career began to take off in the mid-1950s. In 1959, Angelou moved to New York and joined the Harlem Writers Guild. Angelou was active in the Civil Rights Movement, befriending both Malcolm X and Dr. Martin Luther King Jr. Her 1969 memoir *I Know Why the Caged Bird Sings* was the first nonfiction best seller by an African American woman. Angelou published several poetry collections, including 1971's *Just Give Me a Cool Drink of Water 'Fore I Die,* which was nominated for the Pulitzer Prize. At Bill Clinton's 1993 presidential inauguration, she recited her poem "On the Pulse of Morning," the audio version of which later won a Grammy Award for best spoken word album.

A CAGED BIRD

ACTIVIST

ACTRESS

AMAZING PEACE

AND STILL I RISE

ANGELOU

ARKANSAS

AUTHOR

AWARDS

BEST SELLER

BROADWAY

CALYPSO

CAREER

CIVIL RIGHTS

COLLECTION

DANCER

GHANA

GRAMMY

GUILD

HARLEM

LITERATURE

MAYA

MEMOIR

NAACP

NEW YORK

POET

PORGY AND BESS

SCREENPLAY

SINGER

SPOKEN WORD

TONY

WRITER

S A R K A N S A S T R I O M E M
P S Y M M A R G B U O L E G N A
O E E S I R I L L I T S D N A D
K W R E G N I S D O Y N P K A A
E S G U I L D N S R O A S Y M N
N R A U T V A P E I C T M A A C
W E C U V A Y E T A H A B L Z E
O L T G C L R C G G Y R G P I R
R L R P A A E E I A O W K N N A
D E E C C L D R T A X R P E G C
M S S F L B L A D I O I O E P T
E T S O I I N W I Y L T E R E I
L S C R V A A Z W E T E T C A V
R E D I H Y N E A W A R D S C I
A B C G T O N Y A U T H O R E S
H P O R G Y A N D B E S S S V T

Answers on page 183.

MARY TYLER MOORE

Actress Mary Tyler Moore (1936–2017) became a household name when she was cast as Laura Petrie on *The Dick Van Dyke Show*. Moore showed comedic talent and won two Emmys for her performance. When the show ended in 1966, Moore moved on to movies and musicals, including 1967's *Thoroughly Modern Millie* opposite Julie Andrews and 1970's *Change of Habit* with Elvis Presley. *The Mary Tyler Moore Show* debuted in 1970 and was an immediate hit. Moore played the central character, Mary Richards, a single, professional woman living in Minneapolis. The show became a cultural phenomenon, highlighting changing attitudes about women in the workplace. Moore won three Emmys for the sitcom, which ran until 1977. The actress went on to appear in many shows and movies, including 1980's *Ordinary People*, for which she received an Oscar nomination.

ACTRESS

ASNER (Ed)

CAST

CHANGE OF HABIT

COMEDY

DANCER

DICK VAN DYKE

EMMYS

HARPER (Valerie)

KNIGHT (Ted)

LAURA PETRIE

LEACHMAN (Cloris)

MACLEOD (Gavin)

MARY RICHARDS

MARY TYLER MOORE

MINNEAPOLIS

MODERN MILLIE (Thoroughly)

MOVIES

MTM ENTERPRISES

MUSICALS

NOMINATION

ORDINARY PEOPLE

OSCAR

POPULAR

PRODUCER

PROFESSIONAL

ROLE

SHOW

SINGLE

SITCOM

TELEVISION

WHITE (Betty)

WJM-TV

WORKPLACE

```
R R L N M C G T E R M O C T I S L P
F M Q A A D H B E L L Y I V T M J W
E L A S N G S C H W O B I M S P O J
I E T R I O U L S A A R A B Y O R N
L A D N Y D I E A H R R C M L P D O
L C K I O T I S F C Y P T S A U I I
I H V R C V Y O S R I M E U U L N S
M M P P O K E L I E E S N R R A A I
N A T M N G V C E N F O U K A R R V
R N I W N K H A T R I O D M P F Y E
E R D A R A A E N T M A R S E E P L
D A H E R C R H A D N O Y P T L E E
O C N D T P U N C C Y M O J R G O T
M S S R R W I O E D M K X R I N P K
A O E I H M M R V E T U E Y E I L W
F S S I O E C A L P K R O W Y S E O
S E T N D T M I N N E A P O L I S H
S E C Y E J D O E L C A M R I D W S
```

Answers on page 184.

BETTY FORD

After a career as a model and dancer, Betty Ford (1918–2011) married Gerald Ford in 1948, exposing her to the world of politics. Ford became first lady in 1974 when her husband assumed the presidency following Richard Nixon's resignation. Weeks after becoming first lady, Ford was diagnosed with breast cancer and underwent a mastectomy. Ford's openness about her breast cancer battle raised awareness for an illness most Americans were previously reluctant to discuss. Ford was an outspoken supporter of women's rights, equal pay, and abortion rights. Her positions and frankness drew criticism from some conservative Republicans, but she maintained high approval ratings. Ford also spoke openly about her struggles with addiction. In 1982, she founded the Betty Ford Center for substance abuse and addiction and served as its first chair.

ADDICTION	CHAIR	INTERVIEW
ALCOHOLISM	DANCER	MODEL
AMENDMENT	ELIZABETH	MOVEMENT
AWARENESS	EQUAL PAY	NIXON
BETTY	ERA	PRO-CHOICE
BLOOMER	FIRST LADY	RECOVERY
BREAST CANCER	FORD	REPUBLICAN
CAMPAIGN	GERALD	SUBSTANCE ABUSE
CANDID	GRAND RAPIDS	WHITE HOUSE
CENTER	INTERVENTION	

```
N O I T C I D D A V V M U L R A O L
P R O C H O I C E J O N F I I R E C
D E Y G R A T G K T I V A G E D B E
X C S N E W N X I X S H F M O Y C N
P N U O P A E Q O N C I O M A A E T
I A B I U R M N D T M O L L M Q U E
G D S T B E E P S L C C P U O R R
V J T N L N V L N B I O A A H D E R
F T A E I E O K T N H I L X B R C I
I T N V C S M M B O G P P K G O N N
R B C R A S J Z L N A F I H P W A T
S D E E N P E I C Y G W O H A Y C E
T L A T H G S R E C O V E R Y C T R
L A B N T M T N C A N D I D D K S V
A R U I U Y E S U O H E T I H W A I
D E S S E H T E B A Z I L E P Z E E
Y G E R A M E N D M E N T C R F R W
L A C G R A N D R A P I D S Z G B O
```

Answers on page 184.

BILLIE JEAN KING

Billie Jean King (1943–) had a passion for tennis from a young age, and from 1966 through 1975, she was ranked number one in the world six times. In 1973, former men's champion Bobby Riggs declared that even at 55 years old, he could handily beat any female tennis player. In what became known as the "Battle of the Sexes," King and Riggs played in a game broadcast to 90 million television viewers. King won. She used her popularity within the sport to advocate for equal pay and prize money for male and female tennis players. Before retiring in 1990, King won 39 championships, including a record-breaking 20 at Wimbledon. She has remained an advocate for the sport and for gender equality. King was awarded the Presidential Medal of Freedom in 2009.

ADVOCATE

ATHLETE

BATTLE OF THE SEXES

BILLIE JEAN

BOBBY RIGGS

CHAMPION

COMPETE

DOUBLES

EQUAL PAY

FEMALE

GENDER

GRAND SLAM

HALL OF FAME

INTERNATIONAL

KING

MEDAL

MONEY

NUMBER ONE

OPEN

PLAYER

PRIZE

PROFESSIONAL

RANK

SINGLES

SPORT

TENNIS

TITLES

TOURNAMENT

WIMBLEDON

WINNER

WOMEN

```
C I F K C H A M P I O N M G V Z S
O N X E S G G I R Y B B O B S N S
M T W N P P L A Y E R W I E W E D
P E J O R E D N E G O R L I X H J
E R T R I A L B Y M G G M E A S W
T N O E Z D T A E I N B S L E M L
E A U B E V R N M I L E L L N U A
T T R M M O O A S E H O B Q A B N
E I N U X C P A D T F U D N E P O
N O A N R A S O F F O M Y S J S I
N N M T S T N O A D O Z A Y E E S
I A E Y H E E M R N L E P W I L S
S L N S K L E R E E A V L I L T E
S E T G T N E Y I D W A N L I F
U E N T L R A T H O E X U N I T O
Q I A P H R I R E K M N Q E B K R
K B F G R A N D S L A M E R Y O P
```

Answers on page 184.

TONI MORRISON

Toni Morrison (1931–2019) began her career as an English professor at Howard University, but eventually moved to New York City to be a fiction editor for Random House, where she was the first Black woman senior editor for the company. She began informally writing in the late '60s, and over the next few years, Morrison wrote books like *Sula* (1973), which was nominated for a National Book Award, and *Song of Solomon* (1977), which won a National Book Critics Circle Award. Over the next decade, Morrison continued to write and teach; but her 1987 novel *Beloved* would change her life. The book is arguably her most celebrated work, winning the Pulitzer Prize for fiction and inspiring the Oscar-nominated film of the same name. Morrison went on to win the Nobel Prize in literature in 1993, becoming the first African American woman to win the award.

A MERCY	HOWARD	PULITZER
AMERICAN	JAZZ	RANDOM HOUSE
AWARD	LITERATURE	SONG OF SOLOMON
BELOVED	LOVE	
THE BLUEST EYE	MORRISON	SULA
BOOK	NOBEL	TEACH
CHARACTERS	NOVELIST	TONI
CORNELL	PRINCETON	UNIVERSITY
EDITOR	PRIZE	WRITE
FICTION	PROFESSOR	

```
U L O V E E S U O H M O D N A R
R O S S E F O R P D E V O L E B
S W H E Y E T S E U L B E H T J
O E R U T A R E T I L D J J V M
N P Z I S W D J Z N V N D K O O
G E N I T C U R O T L O R H N R
O U D E R E N I A Y T T A C A R
F S O I C P T O C W P E W A C I
S C U B T C M R B T A C O E I S
O O K L I O E Z S E P N H T R O
L R V F A M R I Z Y L I Q U E N
O N Z H A F L B B A S R X Y M T
M E H G A E O X T Y J P O E A O
O L I I V O P U L I T Z E R A N
N L H O K Y T I S R E V I N U I
K P N C C H A R A C T E R S F H
```

Answers on page 184.

GERALDINE FERRARO

Geraldine Ferraro (1935–2011) initially worked as a teacher, but she wanted to pursue a "man's" career instead, so she took night classes at Fordham University to earn a law degree. She worked as an assistant district attorney before being elected to the U.S. House of Representatives in 1978. Ferraro earned a reputation as a rising star in the Democratic Party, focusing her attention on women's rights and urging the passage of the Equal Rights Amendment. When presidential hopeful Walter Mondale chose her to be his running mate in 1984, she was met with sizeable crowds of supporters on the campaign trail. Ferraro became the first woman to receive the vice presidential nomination from either of the two major parties. Although Reagan and Bush won reelection, Ferraro remained active in politics for the rest of her life.

AMENDMENT	DISTRICT	POLITICS
ATTORNEY	ELECTED	REAGAN
BUSH	EQUAL RIGHTS	REPRESENTATIVE
CAMPAIGN	FERRARO	RISING STAR
CAREER	GERALDINE	RUNNING MATE
CHAIR	HOUSE	SPEECH
CONVENTION	MONDALE	TRAIL
CRITIC	NEW YORK	VICE PRESIDENT
CROWDS	NOMINATION	WOMAN
DEMOCRATIC	PARTY	

```
T Q D E T C E L E C R I T I C E P
L I A R T O T N E M D N E M A Q A
Y P O L I T I C S X Z O J E W U R
E V I T A T N E S E R P E R V A T
J D C N A G A E R A R C T I P L Y
C O N V E N T I O N N I C S Z R D
C C R N A X E R Q E S E A D G I N
A I B A O T H N W C P D E H T G O
M T O M T O T Y I R A L W C C H I
P A P R U S O O E D A R I O C T T
A R R S A R G S R D L R E E R S A
I C E W K R I N N N T A E E G C N
G O Z K C D R O I S E P R W R W I
N M V M E S M E I S S Y O E Q G M
W E P N S D U D F C I M Z K G L O
L D T F B U S H Q Y A R Q A Q X N
Z Q P W R U N N I N G M A T E I I
```

Answers on page 185.

DOLLY PARTON

Dolly Parton (1946–) grew up in a poor area of rural Tennessee as one of 12 children. She started singing in church at a young age, and by age 10 she was performing professionally. She moved to Nashville after high school to pursue her career, and she made her album debut in 1967. Parton enjoyed career success throughout the 1970s and '80s, and has continued to record and perform. She has had 25 songs reach number one, has composed over 3,000 songs, and has starred in several movies, including *9 to 5* and *Steel Magnolias*. She has 47 Grammy nominations and was inducted into the Country Music Hall of Fame in 1999. Parton is considered a cultural icon, and her impact on both country and pop music is undeniable.

ACTRESS

ALBUM

ALL I CAN DO

BANJO

BARGAIN STORE
  (The)

BILLBOARD

BLUEGRASS

CATALOG

CHARTS

COMPOSED

COUNTRY

DOLLYWOOD

GRAMMYS

GUITAR

HALL OF FAME

HEARTBREAKER

HERE YOU COME
  AGAIN

I WILL ALWAYS
  LOVE YOU

ICON

JOLENE

JOSHUA

MUSIC

NASHVILLE

PARTON

PHILANTHROPY

PIGEON FORGE

POP

RECORD

SHOW

SOLO

SONGWRITER

STEEL MAGNOLIAS

TRIO

VOCALIST

WAGONER (Porter)

```
G V O C A L I S T Y R T N U O C R E S
P S A I L O N G A M L E E T S E Z T P
D O L L Y W O O D U C R B Z N Y R E I
H X P E E O T I P B L E V O B A N S G
E U E K M R D W Y L F H G A H E G U E R
R D I N A E L N O A R A R C L O R A O
E K I A F T C E A A W G I O I P A U N
Y Y B S F I A A T C A W J X C D M H F
O P L H O R B I T I I S D X O E M S O
U O U V L W U Z N A S L D E N S Y O R
C R E I L G G S O E L R L O D O S J G
O H G L A N T E R L O O T A T P K W E
M T R L H O X T F C O R G R B M V O W
E N A E R S C Z E B A S I U Q O S H H
A A S E M A Q R D P F O B G D C D S U
G L S J O B I L L B O A R D S E S J J
A I W I L L A L W A Y S L O V E Y O U
I H Z M R L L R E K A E R B T R A E H
N P Y D Q O K M U S I C S O J N A B L
```

Answers on page 185.

BARBARA WALTERS

Barbara Walters (1929–) is one of the most famous names in television journalism. In the 1960s and '70s, Walters worked on NBC's *Today* show. By 1972, Walters had proven herself a serious journalist, and accompanied President Nixon on his historic visit to China as part of the press corps. In 1976, she became the first woman to coanchor a network evening news program when she joined the *ABC Evening News*. In 1979, Walters began working on ABC's *20/20*, which she went on to cohost for the next 25 years. Walters interviewed world leaders like the Shah of Iran, Margaret Thatcher, Fidel Castro, and Muammar al-Gaddafi, as well as celebrities like Michael Jackson, Katharine Hepburn, and Sir Laurence Olivier. A record-breaking 74 million viewers watched her 1999 interview of Monica Lewinsky. Walters also cohosted the daytime talk show *The View* from 1997 until 2014.

ABC

ANCHOR

BEGIN (Menachem)

CASTRO (Fidel)

CHINA

COHOST

DAYTIME

DEBATE

EVENING

EXCLUSIVE

GADDAFI (Muammar)

HEPBURN (Katharine)

HUGH DOWNS

INTERVIEW

JACKSON (Michael)

JOURNALIST

LEADERS

LEWINSKY (Monica)

NBC

NEWS

NIXON (Richard)

OLIVIER (Laurence)

ON-AIR

PERSONAL

PRESIDENTS

QUESTION

REEVE (Christopher)

SADAT (Anwar)

SPECIAL

THATCHER (Margaret)

TODAY

TRUMP (Donald)

VIEW (The)

```
E S P E C I A L N E W S Q T I J
R E H C T A H T T R U M P O R K
J L E W I N S K Y R B R A D O Q
J O U R N A L I S T E B W A H E
N I X O N B H E O S C W E Y C M
A N I H C E M L I S O E I E N I
E N C Z P I I D S R N X V V A T
G B O B A V E N Y E A C R E L Y
N Z U I I N W V P D I L E N F A
J R J E T O R E I A R U T I C D
N A R S D S R E C E S S N N A T
B S C H Z S E O E L W I I G S A
U E G K O R H U T V V V P N T D
R U G N S O B C Q Y E E V V R A
H T A I S O N E T A B E D A O S
H L E T N I N I F A D D A G J W
```

Answers on page 185.

SANDRA DAY O'CONNOR

Sandra Day O'Connor (1930–) studied economics at Stanford University and then attended the university's law school, graduating in 1952. O'Connor and her husband settled in Arizona, where O'Connor worked in private practice. She then worked as the state's assistant attorney general. In 1969, Governor Jack Williams appointed her to fill a vacancy in the Arizona state senate; she won reelection twice. O'Connor served on the Maricopa County Superior Court and Arizona's court of appeals before Ronald Reagan nominated her to the Supreme Court in 1981. O'Connor became the first female justice on the nation's highest court after being unanimously confirmed by the Senate. She was a key swing vote in several important cases, including *Planned Parenthood v. Casey*, which upheld *Roe v. Wade*, and *Bush v. Gore*. O'Connor retired in 2006 after serving on the high court for 24 years.

APPEALS	ECONOMICS	O'CONNOR
ARIZONA	FEMALE	REAGAN
ASSOCIATE	FIRST	REPUBLICAN
ATTORNEY GENERAL	ICIVICS	SANDRA DAY
	JUDGE	SENATE
BENCH	JUSTICE	STANFORD
BUSH V. GORE	LAWYER	STATE
CASE	MARICOPA COUNTY	SUPREME
CONFIRMED		SWING VOTE
COURT	MODERATE	

```
A E C W A N O Z I R A S Q P V H
V T S O E J P E G C C N O W Y C
I Z T A N X U E T I E F S T I N
N A Y O C F T S M A F T N H X E
S N P N R A I O T S I U A I D B
T A J P N N R W I O C C T F C
A C T E E O E I M C C I O N S E
N I S L C A N Y A E V E A S L E
F L R E A G L P G I D G H A S T
O B I K V N O S C E A T M G C A
R U F O L C T S G E N E P B O R
D P T B I N F D R S F E J M U E
G E C R M B U S H V G O R E R D
M R A U D J O C O N N O R A T O
K M Y A D A R D N A S Q G S L M
Q K R E Y W A L X S U P R E M E
```

Answers on page 185.

JANE FONDA

The daughter of acclaimed actor Henry Fonda, Jane Fonda (1937–) made her film debut in 1960's *Tall Story* and worked steadily in movies throughout the next three decades, winning Oscars for 1971's *Klute* and 1978's *Coming Home*. Fonda costarred with her father in 1982's *On Golden Pond*. Around this time, Fonda launched a second career with a series of successful aerobic-exercise videos. Fonda is also known for her political activism. She supported civil rights and vociferously opposed the Vietnam War, receiving the nickname "Hanoi Jane" after a trip to North Vietnam. Fonda returned to acting in the mid-2000s, starring in films like *Monster-in-Law, Youth*, and *This Is Where I Leave You*, and shows like *The Newsroom* and *Grace and Frankie*. She continues to be involved in political, environmental, and social movements.

ACTIVIST	COUNTRY GIRL (The)	NEWSROOM (The)
ACTORS STUDIO	EXERCISE	ON GOLDEN POND
ACTRESS	FILM	OSCAR
AEROBICS	FONDA	POLITICAL
ANTI-WAR	GRACE AND FRANKIE	PROTEST
BARBARELLA	HANOI	STAGE
BUTLER (The)	HENRY	TALL STORY
CHAPMAN REPORT (The)	JANE	THEATER
	JULIA	VIDEOS
CHINA SYNDROME (The)	KLUTE	VIETNAM
CLIMATE CHANGE	MONSTER-IN-LAW	WORKOUT
COMING HOME	MY LIFE SO FAR	YOUTH

```
G O D N O P N E D L O G N O O E S I
P G S H E N R Y T U O K R O W C R M
F O R S B A R B A R E L L A I A T F
M O L A E X E R C I S E B B F R D R
O A N I C R V I D E O S O O U X E A
N T I D T E T T M O O R S W E N C E
S Y R L A I A C Y K E E N G A T A M
T C O O U C C N A A F R N J O N A O
E O T U P J O A D I V A N R T C C R
R M S A T E X U L F H N S I T K Y D
I I E R H H R Y N C R S W I W L R N
N N T E A X M N E T T A V T R U O Y
L G O L N H H T A U R I N A M T T S
A H R T O W A S D M S Y C K L E S A
W O P U I M T I A T P S G L I Z L N
W M F B I A O O J Q O A T I F E L I
O E X L G Y R R E T A E H T R B A H
M T C E M A N T E I V E A C K L T C
```

Answers on page 186.

SALLY RIDE

Sally Ride (1951–2012) grew up in Los Angeles and attended Stanford University, where she earned bachelor's degrees in both English and physics. Ride continued studying physics at Stanford, earning a master's degree and a PhD. In 1978, Ride beat out 1,000 other applicants for a spot in NASA's astronaut program. On June 18, 1983, Ride became the first American woman in space aboard the space shuttle *Challenger*. Ride travelled to space again in 1984, and was scheduled for a third trip; sadly, the *Challenger* disaster on January 28, 1986, grounded her permanently. She served on commissions investigating the *Challenger* and *Columbia* disasters. After NASA, Ride became the director of the California Space Institute at the University of California, San Diego, and taught physics at the school. In 2001, she founded Sally Ride Science to inspire girls to pursue careers in science and math.

APPLICANT	MASTERS	SAN DIEGO
ASTRONAUT	MATH	SCIENCE
CALIFORNIA	MISSION	SHUTTLE
CHALLENGER	NASA	SPACE
COLUMBIA	PANEL	STANFORD
COMMISSION	PHD	STEM
EDUCATION	PHYSICS	TRAILBLAZER
FIRST	PROGRAM	UNIVERSITY
INSPIRE	RIDE	WOMAN
LOS ANGELES	SALLY	

```
U E C A P S F L E N A P E S A I
N M E T S M M T S R I F T C T X
K H H W S A N D I E G O H I N J
A I N R O F I L A C K A E E A R
U N I V E R S I T Y L J L N C M
P U O H R E D I R L T S T C I Q
N C L I O T W M E H A Q T E L M
O O O S T Z U N A L W Y U W P A
I M S T N A G A L S I I H O P R
S M A A A E C Y N N T H S M A G
S I N N R S B U S O T E B A J O
I S G F W G A P D A R K R N S R
M S E O X P I N M E T T U S R P
L I L R H R K N J P H Y S I C S
K O E D E R E Z A L B L I A R T
W N S C O L U M B I A G B S M M
```

Answers on page 186.

MAYA LIN

While studying architecture at Yale University in 1981, Maya Lin (1959–) entered a public competition to design the Vietnam Veterans Memorial. Lin, the daughter of Chinese immigrants, incorporated her love of the environment into her design, creating a simple memorial that rises from the earth around it. Surprisingly, the inexperienced 21-year-old architect beat out 1,421 other hopefuls, submitting the winning entry. Some were critical of her minimalist design early on, but today, the Vietnam Veterans Memorial is the most visited war memorial in the country. Lin went on to design the Civil Rights Memorial in Montgomery, Alabama, the Women's Table at Yale, numerous art installations, earthworks, and sculptures in locations around the world. In 2016, she received the Presidential Medal of Freedom–the highest civilian award in the United States.

ABOVE AND BELOW	FINN JUHL	MUSEUM
ARCHITECTURE	FOLD	OHIO
AWARD	FREEDOM	PRESIDENTIAL
BOUNDARIES	GALLERY	PROJECT
CIVIL RIGHTS	GARDEN	ROME
CONFLUENCE	GROUNDSWELL	SCULPTURE
CONTEST	INSTALLATION	VIETNAM VETERANS
DESIGN	MAYA LIN	WAVE FIELD
EARTHWORK	MEDAL	WHAT IS MISSING?
ENVIRONMENT	MEMORIAL	WOMEN'S TABLE
FIELD	MINIMALIST	

```
M G D L O F N G R O U N D S W E L L R
B L A C I V I L R I G H T S M E D A L
V D E D L E I F P M E M O R I A L V D
S I T R P R O J E C T C S H I J R C L
O T E R U B M N U J K E N A W A R D E
H W I T O T L E M T I R K G I V R K I
I T G B N M C U R R S U O N I W C W F
O N N K A A E E A U C I S W O S O D E
Y E I F Y S M D T O T T L L H M E O V
Z M S F U R N V N I A P E A E T L D A
F N S M I U E T E L H B L N M H R L W
R O I S O N E L L T D C S U A I N A Y
E R M B F S N A L N E T R P C T N G E
E I S M T C T J A A A R R A C S W I D
D V I F O I C E U B G M A Y A L I N M
O N T L O N V G L H Y W B N E D R A G
M E A N G O U E W C L V A R S K C V E
I N H D B V I E C N E U L F N O C U Y
L X W A L A I T N E D I S E R P G T H
```

Answers on page 186.

WINONA LADUKE

Winona LaDuke (1959–) is a Native American activist, economist, and author. Her father was a vocal advocate for the Ojibwe people, which greatly influenced LaDuke as child. At 18, she spoke at the United Nations about exploitation of Indian lands. LaDuke earned an economics degree from Harvard, and in 1982 accepted a position as principal of the high school at the White Earth Ojibwe reservation in Minnesota. In 1989, she founded the White Earth Land Recovery Project, which seeks to buy back reservation land from non-Native people, foster sustainable development, and provide economic opportunity. In 1993, LaDuke founded Honor the Earth, which uses music, art, and media to raise funds and support for indigenous environmental issues, such as the Dakota Access Pipeline controversy. LaDuke also ran as the vice-presidential candidate with Ralph Nader on the Green Party ticket in 1996 and 2000.

ACTIVIST	HONOR THE EARTH	PROJECT
ADVOCATE	INDIGENOUS	PROTEST
AUTHOR	INDIGO GIRLS	RECOVERY
CLAIMS	LADUKE	RESERVATION
COFOUNDER	LAND	SCHOOL
DAKOTA ACCESS	LAWSUIT	TRIBAL
ECONOMIST	MINNESOTA	UNITED NATIONS
ENVIRONMENT	NATIVE AMERICAN	WHITE EARTH
GREEN PARTY	OJIBWE	WINONA
HARVARD	PIPELINE	
HEMP	PRINCIPAL	

```
W E T A C O V D A F P D F N Q L F U
F T S E T O R P L W F M O O A A N K
I N D I G E N O U S B I E P E I C P
I A A U T H O R E C T X I H T U O G
N C H C M H H K H A L C K E J P F R
D I I T C I U K V A N A D Q I H O E
I R T S R D E R T I R N I P J T U E
G E L C A A E N R I A V E M O R N N
O M N L E S E P V T U L A J S A D P
G A A G E J C E I I I S I R A E E A
I E T R Q K O O H N R B W K D E R R
R V O S W P N R E T W O M A D T Q T
L I S R N S U Q P E R L N L L I A Y
S T E R E C O V E R Y O A M X H C U
I A N E C O N O M I S T N B E W W P
C N N A N T S I V I T C A O I N O H
D A I L A N D W I N O N A Z H R T A
X N M D A K O T A A C C E S S P T A
```

Answers on page 186.

123

ANITA HILL

Anita Hill (1956–) grew up in Oklahoma and attended Yale Law School, obtaining her Juris Doctor degree in 1980. She began working for Clarence Thomas at the U.S. Department of Education's Office of Civil Rights and later at the Equal Employment Opportunity Commission. Hill left her job and accepted a teaching position in Oklahoma. In 1989, she became the University of Oklahoma College of Law's first tenured Black professor. Hill was thrust into the national spotlight in 1991. After Thomas was nominated to the Supreme Court, Hill testified before the Senate Judiciary Committee that he had sexually harassed her. Although Thomas was ultimately confirmed, Hill's courageous testimony inspired a record number of women to enter politics in 1992, which became known as the "Year of the Woman." Hill now teaches at Brandeis University.

ANITA

ATTORNEY

BLACK

BRANDEIS

CIVIL RIGHTS

COLLEGE

COMMITTEE

CONFIRMATION

DISCRIMINATION

EMPLOYMENT

HEARINGS

HILL

JUDICIARY

LAW

OFFICE

OKLAHOMA

OPPORTUNITY

PROFESSOR

SENATE

SEXUAL HARASSMENT

SPOTLIGHT

SUPREME COURT

TEACH

TENURED

TESTIMONY

THOMAS

UNIVERSITY

WORK

WORKPLACE

YALE

YEAR OF THE WOMAN

```
N L N Q Y T N E M Y O L P M E F Y
H C A S T E S T I M O N Y A D T T
E O M U Y E T A N E S S M S N K I
A M O P R B L A C K A O I E R R N
R M W R A D F B Y M H E M O S C U
I I E E I E Q E O A D S W T O E T
N T H M C R V H L N S U H N S F R
G T T E I U T K A A N G F P E P O
S E F C D N O R R I I O C R C P
Y E O O U E B A V R R T A O O Y P
A S R U J T H E L M L L F L W E O
N E A R Q L R I A I P E L L A N T
I L E T A S V T G K S E B I L R E
T A Y U I I I H R S G A K H C O A
A Y X T C O T O O E L M J B S T C
J E Y K N D W R Q O F F I C E T H
S N O I T A N I M I R C S I D A I
```

Answers on page 187.

MAE JEMISON

After receiving her M.D. from Cornell University in 1977, Mae Jemison (1956–) worked as a Peace Corps medical officer. When she returned to the U.S., she decided to apply to the NASA astronaut training program. In 1987, she became the first Black woman admitted to the program. On September 12, 1992, Jemison became the first African American woman in space aboard the space shuttle *Endeavour*. She is the recipient of numerous awards such as the Essence Science and Technology Award, the Ebony Black Achievement Award, and a Montgomery Fellowship from Dartmouth College. She also established the Jemison Group, which researches, develops, and markets advanced technologies. Jemison is currently the principal of the 100 Year Starship Project, which works to ensure human space travel to another star will be possible by 2112.

AFRICAN AMERICAN	ENDEAVOUR	PRINCIPAL
ASTRONAUT	FIRST	PROGRAM
AWARDS	GROUP	PROJECT
BOARD	HONORS	SHUTTLE
CAMPS	JEMISON	SPACE TRAVEL
CHICAGO	MAE	SPEAKER
CHILDREN'S BOOKS	MEDICAL	SPECIALIST
CORNELL	MISSION	STAR TREK
DARTMOUTH	NASA	STARSHIP
DOCTOR	PEACE CORPS	TEXAS
EBONY	PHYSICIAN	UNIVERSITY

```
R S C S S K O O B S N E R D L I H C
N H T U O M T R A D R S Z X N B T C C
E A S P E A K E R A Z N H A B Y S A
M O C K E R T R A T S R S U I I R M
K I Y I Q N P X P W T A F X T S I P
B P S C R U N I V E R S I T Y T F S
W C Z S I E H L E Y S H N A K B L I
P H C O I S M M A P M A E P O S Z E
B E A E R O A A A C I J R A G P E T
P D A A N R N C N C I I R S A E T D
R T T C G D E N I A N D I H C C U O
O S C O E T E S O C C A E H I I A C
J V R O R C Y A I S W I O M H A N T
E P T A R H O P V A I N R I C L O O
C M V E P N A R R O O M D F S I R R
T E E A X L E D P R U B E O A S T H
L G Q R M A S L S S E R D J Z T S B
Y Y N O B E S P L L G R O U P R A Z
```

Answers on page 187.

RUTH BADER GINSBURG

Ruth Bader Ginsburg (1933–2020), affectionately called "R.B.G." by supporters, was born in Brooklyn to working-class parents who emphasized the value of education. After graduating first in her class at Cornell University, Ginsburg enrolled in Harvard Law School in 1956, where she faced criticism and hostility as one of only nine women in a class of 500 students. She transferred to Columbia University, where she earned a Juris Doctor degree in 1959. Ginsburg taught at Rutgers University Law School and at Columbia, where she became the first female tenured professor. During the 1970s, Ginsburg argued several landmark cases on gender equality before the Supreme Court. In 1980, Jimmy Carter appointed Ginsburg to the U.S. Court of Appeals for the District of Columbia, and in 1993, Bill Clinton nominated her to the Supreme Court. She became the second woman and the first Jewish woman to serve on the Supreme Court.

APPEALS	COLUMBIA	GINSBURG	PROFESSOR
ARGUED	CORNELL	HARVARD	R.B.G.
BADER	COURT	JEWISH	RUTGERS
BROOKLYN	DECISION	JUSTICE	RUTH
CARTER	DISSENT	LIBERAL	SEXISM
CASES	DISTRICT	MARTIN	SUPREME
CIVIL RIGHTS	EDUCATION	MY OWN WORDS	WOMAN
CLINTON	GENDER EQUALITY	OPINION	

```
D I S S E N T G C R N C U S B K
A R G U E D C E A U I N M T A G
N G L M I E H N R T T O L H D H
A B L Y G C E D T G R I I G E N
M R E O L I M E E E A N B I R O
O B N W C S E R R R M I E R E T
W R R N L I R E A S T P R L C C
N O O W I O P Q Z P M O A I I I
O O C O N N U U T G P T L V T R
I K J R T C S A F W E E M I S T
T L E D O C O L U M B I A C U S
A Y W S N E F I C A S E S L J I
C N I C X H R T T R U O C E S D
U M S I X E S Y H A R V A R D H
D U H X H S R O S S E F O R P K
E M G I N S B U R G Z M R U T H
```

Answers on page 187.

NORA EPHRON

The daughter of playwrights, Nora Ephron (1941–2012) created some of film's most beloved characters. Before filmmaking, Ephron worked as a journalist, reporting for the *New York Post* and frequently contributing to *Esquire* magazine. In 1979, while pregnant with her second child, Ephron discovered her husband was having an affair. This prompted her to write her first novel, *Heartburn*, which was later made into a film. Soon after, she launched her screenwriting career with the script for the film *Silkwood*. But it was Ephron's next screenplay for *When Harry Met Sally* that elevated her fame in Hollywood and secured her place as a leader in the romantic comedy genre. She wrote and directed *Sleepless in Seattle, You've Got Mail*, and *Julie & Julia*.

AFFAIR	HEARTBURN	SCREENWRITER
CHARACTERS	HOLLYWOOD	SEATTLE
COMEDY	JULIA	SILKWOOD
CRAZY SALAD	JULIE	SLEEPLESS
DIRECTOR	MEG RYAN	TOM HANKS
EPHRON	NEW YORK POST	WALLFLOWER
ESQUIRE	NORA	WHEN HARRY MET SALLY
ESSAYS	NOVEL	YOU'VE GOT MAIL
FILM	PLAY	
GENRE	ROMANTIC	

```
T S C R E E N W R I T E R C G M B U
V W N S S E L P E E L S O J V P D A
C R A Z Y S A L A D V M J W D J L V
W H E N H A R R Y M E T S A L L Y S
V J T G E R N E G D C N A Y R G E M
F N V D C N E W Y O R K P O S T P N
S R E T C A R A H C U O U T Y R H R
T H R W Y S I E T Q E U C R O S E F
D S E T L L E M P R V I N B U Y A S
I H W E U K M A I H M M X J V A R F
R D O J C U K U T R R L H L E S T Y
E O L L G I Q O W T I O I L G S B R
C O F B L S T T E B L A N F O E U M
T W L P E Y D N Y N B E F M T N R E
O K L D Z D W A A H O Y V F M O N I
R L A M R C L O Q M Z V I E A R K L
L I W F C P M T O K O U E F I A L U
U S K N A H M O T D E R S L L Q S J
```

Answers on page 187.

MADELEINE ALBRIGHT

As a child, Madeleine Albright (1937–) fled Prague when the Nazis invaded at the beginning of World War II. After the war, she and her family immigrated to the United States, eventually settling in Denver, Colorado. Albright received a PhD in public law and government from Columbia University in 1976. She began a political career working for Senator Edward Muskie and for National Security Advisor Zbigniew Brzezinski during the Carter administration, and then became a professor of international affairs at Georgetown University. In 1992, President Bill Clinton appointed Albright to be the U.S. representative to the United Nations. In 1996, Clinton nominated Albright for secretary of state, and she became the first woman to ever hold the position. As secretary of state, Albright advocated for human rights around the world. In May 2012, she was awarded the Presidential Medal of Freedom.

ADVISOR	GEORGETOWN	POLITICAL
ALBRIGHT	GOVERNMENT	PRAGUE
APPOINTED	THE HAGUE	PROFESSOR
CARTER	HUMAN RIGHTS	RELATIONS
CLINTON	INTERNATIONAL	SECRETARY
COLUMBIA	LAW	STATE
COUNCIL	MADELEINE	UNITED NATIONS
DEMOCRACY	MUSKIE	WOMAN
DEPARTMENT	NATIONAL SECURITY	WORLD
DIPLOMAT	NAZIS	
FOREIGN	NOMINATED	

```
T C L I N T O N E U G A H E H T P U
J N D S Q A E I Y R A T E R C E S R
B Z E W N I N C G S I Z A N N F R X
E G A M K O A E N I E L E D A M X E
T L S S N R I P W C O T C Q T N C C
A I U D C R C T H O A C S E I G T O
T M N O E O E Q A M M N W D O E V L
S L M T U P A V O L O A T E N O S U
T E A N E D A L O I E P N T A R T M
D H C C V R P R T G R R N N L G H B
W I G I I I N A T O R O M I S E G I
L C S I D T N A F M M T F O E T I A
T O A S R D I E T I E O Q P C O R E
R W D R E B S L N I R N C P U W N J
I E O T T S L A O E O E T A R N A V
D A I R O E T A I P Z N L R I D M X
H N L R L E R G R T W E A E T M U N
U H U N D D N E U G A R P L Y O H S
```

Answers on page 188.

OPRAH WINFREY

In 1983, Oprah Winfrey (1954–) took a job at a low-rated morning talk show, *A.M. Chicago*. Within months, the ratings skyrocketed. In 1986, it was relaunched as *The Oprah Winfrey Show* and picked up nationally. Produced and hosted by its namesake, *Oprah* aired for 25 seasons and remains the highest-rated daytime talk show in American history. In 2011, Winfrey launched the Oprah Winfrey Network (OWN). Winfrey also acted in films such as *The Color Purple, Beloved, Selma*, and *A Wrinkle in Time*. One of the first Black female billionaires, Winfrey is also well known for her philanthropy. She has appeared in *Time*'s most influential people list ten times and won many accolades, including Daytime and Primetime Emmys, a Peabody, multiple NAACP Image Awards, the Presidential Medal of Freedom, and the Golden Globes' Cecil B. DeMille Award for lifetime achievement.

ACTRESS	EMMYS	MEDIA	RATINGS
AWARD	EXECUTIVE	MOGUL	SEASONS
BELOVED	FAVORITE THINGS	NAACP IMAGE	SELMA
BILLIONAIRE		OBAMA	SPIN-OFFS
BOOK CLUB	GIVEAWAYS	OPRAH	STUDIOS
CECIL B. DEMILLE	GUESTS	OWN	TALK SHOW
	HARPO	PEABODY	TELEVISION
CHICAGO	HOST	PHILANTHROPY	WINFREY
COLOR PURPLE (The)	INTERVIEW	PRODUCER	
	MAGAZINE	PRODUCTIONS	
DAYTIME			

```
T H A R P O J Y E M M Y S N O S A E S
W O H S K L A T E N I Z A G A M Y X Q
G O N X E L P R U P R O L O C F M X E
Y E O S S E L M A B S T U D I O S R C
J L Y G F L T E L E V I S I O N I P T
Q L E N A Z S R M L A W A R D A I H R
W I R I V C A I N O P S F O N L R O D
E M F T O E I S O V G N Q O X E P A P
I E N A R S K H K E T U I G C R Y A H
V D I R I N R E C D S L L U A T C S I
R B W S T O M G C O L T D H I T E P L
E L P Y E I B A X I H O S M R R X I A
T I E A T T U M B E R H E E P V E N N
N C A W H C L I I P C D S M U L C O T
I E B A I U C P D A H S E H O G U F H
C C O E N D K C D S M D V O N V T F R
Q Q D V G O O A G Q I A U S L R I S O
E V Y I S R O A K A X F B T I G V G P
R W C G C P B N T Y O W N O S V E C Y
```

Answers on page 188.

CONDOLEEZZA RICE

Condoleezza Rice (1954–) dreamed of becoming a concert pianist. She initially majored in music at the University of Denver, but ended up graduating with a degree in political science. Rice earned her master's from the University of Notre Dame in 1975 and her PhD in international studies from the University of Denver in 1981. That same year, she joined Stanford University as a professor. An expert on the Soviet Union, Rice worked on the National Security Council in the late-1980s. In 1993, after returning to Stanford, Rice became the first woman and first African American to serve as provost of the university. From 2001 until 2005, Rice served as the first woman national security advisor under President George W. Bush. In Bush's second term, Rice became the first Black woman to serve as secretary of state. In 2012, Rice became one of the first female members of the Augusta National Golf Club.

ADVISOR	EXPERT	POLITICAL SCIENCE
AFRICAN AMERICAN	FELLOW	PROFESSOR
ALABAMA	FIRST	PROVOST
AUGUSTA	GOLF CLUB	RICE
BLACK	GOVERNMENT	SECRETARY
BUSH	INTERNATIONAL	SOVIET UNION
CONDOLEEZZA	IRAQ	STANFORD
COUNCIL	MIDDLE EAST	STATE
DEMOCRACY	NATIONAL SECURITY	TRANSFORMATIONAL
DENVER	NOTRE DAME	UNIVERSITY
DIPLOMAT	PIANO	WOMAN

```
T R E P X E L G T S R I F Y P C B C O
C R Y N E D R O F N A T S W O Q D N P
C O A T O T S A A R J P H N F E A O K
S L U N I T A E S M G M D L N I L G Q
A E A N S R R T C O A O V V P I P O V
C F C N C F U E S R L B E M T A R L B
Y T R I O I O C D E E R A I S T O F U
C N D I R I L R E A T T C L N S F C S
A E W T C F T Z M S M A A P A U E L H
R M D R D A Z A O A L E M R Y G S U M
C N I U O A N V N S T A J B Y U S B I
O R P Q X S O A C R J I N G L A O E D
M E L A C R I I M U E W O O R A R Y D
E V O R P T E V B E Y T O N I Y C L L
D O M I E N V M D G R K N M A T P K E
V G A O C G X M B A J I K I A L A U E
M R T E F E L L O W Y D C L D N P N A
A Y T I S R E V I N U P E A N G Q F S
Z V N O I N U T E I V O S Y N Z T F T
```

Answers on page 188.

KATIE COURIC

Katie Couric (1957–) became interested in journalism at an early age. She landed her first job as a desk assistant at ABC. In 1989, with her career taking off, Couric began working as a reporter at the Pentagon. She also began filling in as cohost on NBC's morning show, *Today*, where she was an instant hit. Couric remained on the show for 15 years, until 2006. That year, Couric made her debut on the *CBS Evening News*, becoming the first woman to anchor the program solo. She also contributed to *60 Minutes* and anchored primetime news specials, earning a salary of $15 million a year–making her one of the highest paid journalists in the world. Couric has also written books including *The Brand New Kid, The Blue Ribbon Day,* and *The Best Advice I Ever Got: Lessons from Extraordinary Lives.*

ABC	CONTRIBUTOR	MORNING
ADVICE	COURIC	NEWS
ANCHOR	EVENING	PENTAGON
BLUE RIBBON DAY (The)	EXTRAORDINARY	PROGRAM
	GLOBAL	REPORTER
BRAND NEW KID (The)	HOSTS	SHOW
BROADCAST	INTERVIEW	SPECIALS
CAREER	JOB	TODAY
CBS	JOURNALISM	TV PERSONALITY
COHOST	KATIE	WASHINGTON
COLONOSCOPY	LESSONS	YAHOO
	LIVES	

M C O N T R I B U T O R G O T O Z W
Z Q T B L C M O R N I N G L U S V A
E R C R N O C T U M Q P U S O O B I
X E Y A E U V C K W O H S I B B O L
T T P N W R I S P E C I A L S C A I
R R O D S I J O U R N A L I S M X L
A O C N F C C R Z U B E C I V D A T
O P S E B L U E R I B B O N D A Y K
R E O W L T E B C W E I V R E T N I
D R N K T V P E R S O N A L I T Y Z
I T O I A J G N N O S U E X I C Y I
N O L D S N O O Y T A T S O H O C R
A D O E I G S A S P J D R O C E Y E
R A C N A S N O Q O K C C S S H C E
Y Y E T E C H D B E V A B A E G P R
C V N L H W I Y A H O O T A S V V A
E E N O T G N I H S A W F I T T I C
P I R S M A R G O R P F P X E I L L

Answers on page 188.

KATHRYN BIGELOW

In 2009, Kathryn Bigelow (1951–) won the Academy Award for best director for *The Hurt Locker*, becoming the first woman to receive this honor. In a strange twist of fate, Bigelow was up against her ex-husband James Cameron in the best director and best picture categories that year. Bigelow took both categories, and *The Hurt Locker* won four additional Oscars. Bigelow directed her first feature film, *The Loveless*, in 1981. She followed up with 1987's *Near Dark* and 1989's *Blue Steel*. But it was 1991's *Point Break*, starring Keanu Reeves and Patrick Swayze, that proved to be Bigelow's break into mainstream filmmaking. Bigelow's directing credits include *The Weight of Water* (2000), *K-19: The Widowmaker* (2002), *The Hurt Locker* (2008), which followed members of a bomb squad in the Iraq War, *Zero Dark Thirty* (2012), which depicted American efforts to find Osama bin Laden, and *Detroit* (2017).

ACTION

AWARDS

BAFTA

BIGELOW

BLUE STEEL

BOMB SQUAD

CRITICS

DETROIT

DIRECTOR

FILMMAKER

HURT LOCKER (The)

IRAQ WAR

KATHRYN

LOVELESS (The)

MARK BOAL

MOVIE

NEAR DARK

OSAMA BIN LADEN

OSCAR

POINT BREAK

PRODUCER

SCREENWRITER

STRANGE DAYS

TORTURE

WEIGHT OF WATER (The)

WIDOWMAKER (The)

WOMAN

ZERO DARK THIRTY

```
F I L M M A K E R E R U T R O T W
B Z Y Y W E I G H T O F W A T E R
I X G K U X D R E C U D O R P V R
G M Y X A P R E K A M W O D I W K
E S O T N E D A L N I B A M A S O
L B T V R B R J L O V E L E S S W
O O B R I I E B R O D F D I C P O
W M Z R A E H A T E F B T R R D M
A B P A G N C T T N L P N E E I A
W S L W N S G R K U I Y W K E R N
A Q A Q O E O E E R R O S C N E S
R U O A A I A S D H A C P O W C A
D A B R T C T R T A I D B L R T W
S D K I L E T A D T Y A O T I O J
W T R O E U K I I A F S I R T R R
E L A L L Q J R O T R M V U E O R
U E M K N T C P A N Y K R H R Z Y
```

Answers on page 189.

HILLARY CLINTON

Hillary Clinton (1947–) was active in politics at a young age, participating in student council and serving as class vice president in high school. After graduating from Yale Law School, she married fellow graduate Bill Clinton, who was elected governor of Arkansas in 1978 and reelected four times. Clinton served as first lady from 1993 until 2001. After leaving the White House, Clinton became the first woman elected to the U.S. Senate from New York. In early 2007, she announced her candidacy for president. Clinton lost in the Democratic Primary to Barack Obama, who went on to win the presidency. Clinton served as Obama's secretary of state from 2009 until 2013. In 2016, Clinton became the first woman to be the presidential nominee of a major political party. Although she won the popular vote, Clinton lost the presidential race to Donald Trump in the Electoral College.

ARKANSAS	EDUCATION	RACE
BILL	FAMILY	RODHAM
CAMPAIGN	FIRST LADY	SCANDAL
CHELSEA	HILLARY	SECRETARY
CHILDREN	HUMAN RIGHTS	SENATOR
CLINTON	LAWYER	STATE
COMMITTEE	NEW YORK	WHITE HOUSE
CONGRESS	PARTY	WOMEN'S RIGHTS
DEFENSE FUND	PRESIDENT	YALE
DEMOCRAT	PRIMARY	

```
C O N G R E S S R R O T A N E S
C S A Y D N U F E S N E F E D Q
J L T T R S E V Q W C T O U L A
L C R H R A M L H V H Y F M A R
N T O R G A M I A B E R I S W K
I O T M H I T I D Y L A R T Y A
K N I D M E R E R N S L S H E N
R F O T H I M N G P E L T G R S
O R A O A O T I A U A I L I S A
Y B U M C C A T C M L H A R C S
W S M R I P U A E L U R D S A G
E S A I M L I D I E I H Y N N E
N T P A R T Y B E R B N N E D C
A A C S E C R E T A R Y T M A A
R T P T N E D I S E R P M O L R
N E X C H I L D R E N N I W N S
```

Answers on page 189.

ELLEN DEGENERES

Ellen DeGeneres (1958–) started doing stand-up at age 23. Her routine was a huge hit, and before long she was touring nationally. DeGeneres was invited to appear on *The Tonight Show Starring Johnny Carson* in 1986. Her success on *The Tonight Show* led to a transition from stand-up comedy to sitcom star, and her show *Ellen* debuted in 1994. It was on this show in 1997 that her character–and DeGeneres herself–came out as gay. *Ellen* became the first primetime show with an openly gay character. Despite audience support and an Emmy Award for the coming-out episode, *Ellen* was canceled in 1998. In 2003, she launched *The Ellen DeGeneres Show*, a popular Emmy-winning daytime talk show. She voiced the role of Dory in Pixar's *Finding Nemo* (2003) and *Finding Dory* (2016). DeGeneres has been married to actress Portia de Rossi since 2008.

ACTRESS	EMMY	PRIMETIME
AWARDS	EPISODE	SHOW
COMEDIAN	GAY	SITCOM
COMIC	GUESTS	SPECIAL
COMING OUT	HOST	STAND-UP
CONEHEADS	JOHNNY CARSON	STAR
DANCING	LOVE LETTER (The)	TALK
DAYTIME	MR. WRONG	TONIGHT
DEGENERES	NEMO	TOUR
DORY	NEW ORLEANS	VEGETARIAN
EDTV	PIXAR	VOICE
ELLEN	PORTIA	WILDLIFE

```
N C P O R T I A E P I S O D E R
L O Z R U O T D E G E N E R E S
N A S R E T T E L E V O L N C T
E T I R N E W O R L E A N S E E
M M H C A G N I C N A D V V M S
O R I G E C S D R A W A E M I W
C A Y T I P Y G C D C G Y T V I
O T E S E N S N J O E O C V S L
M S D D G M O G N T M O M S H D
I M A A T U I T A H M E E I S L
N R H E Y V E R R Y O R D T C I
G W O H H T I S P A T J A I Y F
O R S E S A I N T C X N T R A E
U O T N N H V M A S D I O A F N
T N E O E H O J E U S D P I L Y
W G E C I O V W P J E L L E N K
```

Answers on page 189.

SONIA SOTOMAYOR

Sonia Sotomayor (1954–) grew up in Spanish-speaking Puerto Rican neighborhood in the Bronx. A determined child, Sotomayor became fluent in English and decided she would one day be a judge. Sotomayor graduated from Princeton in 1976, then earned a Juris Doctor degree from Yale in 1979. In 1984, she entered private practice and began doing pro bono work for agencies like the Puerto Rican Legal Defense and Education Fund. In 1992, President George H.W. Bush nominated her to be a U.S. District Court Judge for the Southern District of New York, and President Bill Clinton then elevated her to the U.S. Second Circuit Court of Appeals. Sotomayor was nominated to the Supreme Court by President Barack Obama. When she was confirmed in August 2009, she became the first Latina on the highest court in the country, far surpassing her childhood dream.

ACA	EDITOR	OPINION
APPEALS	FUND	PUERTO RICAN
ARGUMENT	JOURNAL	SAME-SEX MARRIAGE
ATTORNEY	JUDGE	
BAR EXAM	JUSTICE	SECOND CIRCUIT
BRONX	LATINA	SONIA
BUSH	LAW	SOTOMAYOR
CLINTON	LEGAL DEFENSE	SUPREME
CONFIRMED	NEW YORK CITY	TRIAL
COURT	NOMINATED	YALE
DISTRICT	OBAMA	

```
N E W Y O R K C I T Y J C S Z L M
R X L X D E M R I F N O C J A V E
B I S O T O M A Y O R T W N T G A
X J Q P U E C J M L A I R O A E P
H N J U Q Y S J U M K U M I A G P
D K O E M A N N A S O C R J N N E
D B A R J L Y B E J T R C U I O A
E N T T B E O V H F A I Z D T I L
T O T O S U P R E M E C C G A N S
A T O R D X U N X T M D V E L I K
N N R I N I M E N G L N L V M P B
I I N C K S S E D E A O M A R O T
M L E A O E M T D Q L C X F G R D
O C Y N M U K I R A U E A P U E P
N L I A G H T I I I R S W O A N L
D A S R N O K R M A C C C L A W D
J E A J R W T T B D W T R H S U B
```

Answers on page 189.

MERYL STREEP

Meryl Streep (1949–) started her acting career on the New York stage in the late 1960s. She transitioned to movies in the 1970s, appearing in films such as *The Deer Hunter* and *Kramer vs. Kramer*, for which Streep received her first Oscar. She won her second Academy Award for her performance in *Sophie's Choice*. Streep received nominations for *Out of Africa* (1985), *Postcards from the Edge* (1990), *The Bridges of Madison County* (1995), *Adaptation* (2002), *The Devil Wears Prada* (2006), *Doubt* (2008), and *Julie & Julia* (2009). Streep won her third Oscar for her portrayal of Margaret Thatcher in 2011's *The Iron Lady*. She garnered a record 20th Academy Award nomination in 2017 for *Florence Foster Jenkins* and starred opposite Tom Hanks in *The Post* later that year. Considered one of the greatest actresses of her generation, Streep continues acting today.

ACADEMY AWARDS

ACTRESS

ADAPTATION

ANGELS IN AMERICA

BIG LITTLE LIES

DEER HUNTER (The)

DEVIL WEARS PRADA (The)

DOUBT

DRAMA

GOLDEN GLOBES

THE HOURS

INTO THE WOODS

IRON LADY (The)

JULIA CHILD

KRAMER VS. KRAMER

LAUNDROMAT (The)

LITTLE WOMEN

MAMMA MIA!

MERYL

NEW YORK

NOMINATIONS

OSCARS

OUT OF AFRICA

PLAYS

THE POST

SCREEN

SOPHIE'S CHOICE

STAGE

STREEP

SUFFRAGETTE

THATCHER (Margaret)

```
D E V I L W E A R S P R A D A D N T L
S N O I T A N I M O N D O S C A R S A
O K E G A T S A H X E D T K M S E O U
W F O I C T S T R E E P A E A E C P N
J N U A D L M B R Y X M I R M B I E D
W O T Q C O N H Z C A N D E M O O H R
T I O A L I U O H R T I U F A L H T O
Q T F S C N R B D O P T D T M G C S M
N A A G T A P E T J H L H S I N S Z A
E T F E Z O D H M A U E A N A E E B T
M P R V I M E E T A H L E Y R D I O K
O A I B K W E C M O N E I T S L H H R
W D C H O H H R U Y R I C A V O P Q O
E A A O H E T R Y C A A S A C G O D Y
L Q D O R X S Q S L F W Y L L H S R W
T S K R A M E R V S K R A M E R I X E
T H D I R O N L A D Y O W R U G A L N
I X N S U F F R A G E T T E D Z N X D
L S E I L E L T T I L G I B A S I A K
```

Answers on page 190.

MICHELLE OBAMA

Growing up on Chicago's South Side, Michelle Obama (1964–) was a hard-working, gifted student. She studied sociology at Princeton University and earned a Juris Doctor degree from Harvard Law School in 1988. She met Barack Obama while working at the Chicago branch of firm Sidley Austin. The two married in 1992. She left corporate law for a career in public service, working as an assistant to the mayor and heading up a nonprofit. When her husband was elected president, Obama became the first African American first lady in U.S. history. During the president's two terms, she was an advocate for women, children, the homeless, and military families. She created the "Let's Move!" initiative to fight childhood obesity. Since leaving the White House, Obama has continued to advocate for a healthier, more inclusive America. Her 2018 memoir *Becoming* was later made into a Netflix documentary of the same name.

BARACK	FAMILIES	MALIA	ROBINSON
BECOMING	FASHION ICON	MICHELLE	SASHA
CHICAGO	FIRST LADY	MILITARY	SIDLEY AUSTIN
CHILDREN	FOOD	NETFLIX	SOCIAL ISSUES
COMMUNITY	GARDEN	NONPROFIT	SOUTH SIDE
CRAIG	HARVARD	OBAMA	WHITE HOUSE
DIRECTOR	HEALTH	OUTREACH	WOMEN
DOCUMENTARY	HOMELESS	PRESIDENT	
EDUCATION	LAWYER	PRINCETON	
EXECUTIVE	LET'S MOVE!	PUBLIC SERVICE	

```
E E D I S H T U O S B E A W G H U
D N O I T A C U D E A W H O N O S
O I Y K C A R A B U R F S M I M E
F I R S T L A D Y S A N A E M E I
L T A E A M A B O S Y I S N O L L
A I T E C I W E H I T T O M C E I
W F N E C T L I H L I S H I E S M
Y O E E V I O A C A N U A L B S A
E R M M V N V R M I U A R I F I F
R P U I I I A R B C M Y V T G T N
L N C C C I T O E O M E A A G N E
E O O H G W R U C S O L R R A E R
T N D E D I R E C T C D D Y R D D
S F Y L E S U O H E T I H W D I L
M O W L N E T F L I X S L S E S I
O O A E O G A C I H C E G B N E H
V D L D O U T R E A C H I L U R C
E H E A L T H N O T E C N I R P A
```

Answers on page 190.

SERENA WILLIAMS

Serena Williams (1981–) began playing tennis at the age of three, practicing for two hours a day with her father. By the time she was nine, she was ranked first in the 10-and-under division on the United States Tennis Association tour. Williams turned pro in 1995 when she was only 14 years old. Williams and her sister, Venus, often played against each other. But in 2002, Williams beat Venus in the finals of Wimbledon, the U.S. Open, and the French Open, and in 2003 she won the Australian Open. After her stellar year, Williams faced personal difficulties, and her ranking fell to 139th. Williams made a comeback in 2008, winning the U.S. Open and regaining her top place in the rankings. Williams has won a total of 23 Grand Slam singles titles, and she and Venus are active in charity work, often teaming up for philanthropic projects.

ATHLETE	FRENCH OPEN	STAR
CAREER	GRAND SLAM	TENNIS
COMEBACK	INJURIES	TITLES
COURT	MATCH	TOUR
DAUGHTER	OLYMPICS	TRAINING
DEFEAT	POWERFUL	U.S. OPEN
DOUBLES	PROFESSIONAL	VENUS
FASHION	RANKINGS	VICTORIES
FATHER	SERENA	WILLIAMS
FINALS	SISTERS	WIMBLEDON

```
T I D L A N O I S S E F O R P E L
L B U O D F R E N C H O P E N R
S R E T S I S E F E D S T A R A
V E N U S V I C T O R I E S N C
N S L A N I F A S H I O N I L W
M A L S D N A R G C G R F F K I
A G S C S J T S T A U U S C E M
T N M I E U H W U O T E A T T B
C I A P R R E T C H L B E D O L
H N I M E I R R G B E L V E U E
F I L Y N E M U U M H E E F R D
A A L L A S A O O T D R R E I O
S R I O F D D C A R E E R A R N
H T W S I N N E T Y W S H T A F
E R A N K I N G S O V A T H L E
T I T L E S P H P N E P O S U F
```

Answers on page 190.

BEYONCÉ

Beyoncé Knowles (1981–) loved music and performing from an early age. She rose to fame in the late 1990s as lead vocalist of all-female group Destiny's Child. They signed with Columbia Records in 1997, and in 1998 Destiny's Child released their first, self-titled album. Their multi-platinum second album, *The Writing's on the Wall*, included such hits as "Bills, Bills, Bills" and "Say My Name." The singer established a solo career with the 2003 release of her debut album, *Dangerously in Love*, which featured her first number-one single, "Crazy in Love." She has also starred in several films, including *Dreamgirls* and *Cadillac Records*. In 2008, Beyoncé married rapper and hip-hop artist Jay-Z. She holds the record for most Grammy Award wins ever by a female artist with 28. Beyoncé is one of the top-selling, most influential entertainers of our time.

AWARDS	DREAMGIRLS	INFLUENTIAL	SASHA FIERCE
BEYONCÉ	EVERYTHING IS LOVE	JAY-Z	SAY MY NAME
BLACK IS KING	GIRL'S TYME	KELLY ROWLAND	SINGLE LADIES
CADILLAC	GRAMMYS	KNOWLES	SOLO
CAREER	GROUP	LEMONADE	SUPER BOWLS
COACHELLA	HALO	OBSESSED	TOURS
COLUMBIA	HOMECOMING	PERFORMER	VISUAL ALBUM
CRAZY IN LOVE	HOUSTON	RECORDS	VOCALIST
DESTINY'S CHILD	INAUGURAL BALL	RELEASE	

```
R S R A W A O B S E S S E D S N S
E E P C A L L I D A C B F D A L A
L L U E M Y T S L R I G R L R U Y
E W O P S L C H L A H A L I M D M
A O R K E L A A A H W E G D M L Y
S N G G I A R L B A H M E N U I N
E K G N D I E O L C A D V A B H A
R T N I A T E S A E R N O L L C M
E S I K L N R O R C E O L W A S E
M I M S E E C D U R C T N O L Y T
R L O I L U O Z G E O S I R A N E
O A C K G L L Y U I R U Y Y U I D
F C E C N F O A A F D O Z L S T A
R O M A I N S J N A S H A L I S N
E V O L S I G N I H T Y R E V E O
P O H B S R U O T S D U C K W D M
K C C O L U M B I A B E Y O N C E
S L W O B R E P U S Y M M A R G L
```

Answers on page 190.

NANCY PELOSI

Nancy Pelosi (1940–) became interested in politics at a young age. She attended Trinity College in Washington, D.C., where she graduated with a degree in political science. She started as a volunteer for the Democratic Party and gradually rose up the ranks. In 1987, Pelosi won a special election for California's Eighth District, and in 2002 she became the first female Democratic leader of the U.S. House of Representatives. Four years later, Pelosi made history again when she was elected Speaker of the House, becoming the first woman ever to hold the speakership. Pelosi was instrumental in helping pass the Affordable Care Act (ACA). She remained House Speaker until 2010, when Republicans regained control of the House. After Democrats won control of the House in the 2018 midterms, Pelosi was again elected House Speaker and continues to be a vocal fighter for her party's values.

BUSH	FIRST	PELOSI
CALIFORNIA	FUNDRAISER	POLITICIAN
CAMPAIGN	HEALTH CARE	REFORM
CONTROL	HOUSE	REPRESENTATIVES
DEMOCRAT	IMPEACHMENT	SAN FRANCISCO
DISTRICT	LEADERSHIP	SPEAKER
EIGHTH	NANCY	TRINITY
ELECTED	OBAMA	TRUMP
FAMILY	PARTY	VOLUNTEER
FEMALE	PASS	WOMAN

```
O B A M A H O T R I N I T Y W O
R E P R E S E N T A T I V E S H
I T E S U O H S U B O F F F U E
S C D C D I S T R I F U Y I B A
O I E A R A A H R C O N T R O L
L R T M P E T E A A N D V S C T
E T C P W H F L P M R R O A S H
P S E A G O I O F P O A L P I C
R I L I R F M I M A F I U P C A
Y D E M O C R A T I I S N A N R
L P A R T N O C N G L E T R A E
I T N S B Y C N A N A R E T R P
M I R E K A E P S H C G E Y F M
A I M P E A C H M E N T R I N U
F E M A L E A D E R S H I P A R
E I G H N A I C I T I L O P S T
```

Answers on page 191.

MELINDA GATES

Melinda Gates (1964–) became interested in computer programming at age 14. After receiving a bachelor's degree in computer science from Duke University and an MBA from Duke's Fuqua School of Business, Gates worked for Microsoft. She married Microsoft CEO Bill Gates in 1994. That year, she and her husband cofounded what would later become the Bill & Melinda Gates Foundation, which works to improve global health and education. Gates also works to encourage more women to join the computing field and to increase workplace diversity, especially in the technology industry. She has frequently been ranked as one of the world's most powerful women by *Forbes*. In 2016, Gates and her husband received the Presidential Medal of Freedom for their philanthropic efforts. The couple announced their decision to divorce in May 2021.

BILL	FOUNDATION	MELINDA
BUSINESS	FREEDOM	MICROSOFT
COCHAIR	FRENCH	MOTHER
COMPUTERS	GATES	PHILANTHROPIST
DEVELOPMENT	GLOBAL	POVERTY
DIVERSITY	HEALTH	POWERFUL
DUKE	INDUSTRY	TECHNOLOGY
EDUCATION	INVESTMENT	VACCINES
EMPOWERMENT	LIFT	WOMEN
FORBES	MEDAL	WORKPLACE

```
F O R B U S I N E S S B I L L D
P O W E R F U L B I L A B O L G
H M O T H E R E M E L I N D A I
I N V E S T M E N T D U K E G N
L I T A C U D E S E B R O F A D
A H P C E O M I C R O S O F T U
N I V O M F R H V A C C I N E S
T N E M P O L E V E D L N N E T
H D H P O U H D G P R E A C I M
R U E U W N C U U A M S A E C O
O S A T E D N C M O T L I O H D
P T L E R A E A W O P E C T H E
I R T R M T R T O K T H S O Y E
S Y H S E I F I R I A H C O C R
T E C H N O L O G Y L A D E M F
T F I L T N W N P O V E R T Y L
```

Answers on page 191.

LADY GAGA

Lady Gaga (1986–) began playing the piano and singing at the age of four. She earned early admission to New York University's Tisch School of the Arts, but eventually withdrew to work on creative projects. She adopted the name "Lady Gaga" in homage to the Queen song "Radio Ga-Ga." Between 2007 and 2008, Gaga wrote and recorded her debut album, *The Fame*, which contained several number one singles, including "Just Dance" and "Poker Face." Since then, Gaga gained acclaim for subsequent albums, including a collaboration with Tony Bennett, as well as her acting skills. She earned a Golden Globe for her role on *American Horror Story* and was nominated for an Oscar for her costarring role in *A Star Is Born*. Lady Gaga is an outspoken advocate for LGBTQ rights around the world, youth empowerment, and anti-bullying campaigns.

A STAR IS BORN	THE FAME	OSCAR
ACTING	FASHION	PIANO
ADVOCATE	GOLDEN GLOBE	POKER FACE
ALBUM	GRAMMY	POP
ANTI-BULLYING	ICON	SINGER
BORN THIS WAY	JOANNE	SUPER BOWL
CHEEK TO CHEEK	JUST DANCE	TONY BENNETT
CHROMATICA	LADY GAGA	YOUTH
DEBUT	LGBTQ RIGHTS	

```
A D V O C A T E O Y O U T H A J
S T H G I R Q T B G L P O P C R
T E N O C I B O R N T H I S T P
A N A L O F B N E I R E G N I S
R N O D U A F Y P Y I H S A F K
I A J E E S N B U L O P N Y E J
S O S N C H Y E S L S O A E U G
B J A G A I M N O U F W H S N I
O I G L F O M N P B S C T I A R
R C A O R N A E L I O D T D D Q
N O G B E F R T H T A C H E T T
A M Y E K B G T K N A I P B S B
F U D G O E N E C A U G G U U G
E B A W P R E E O S C A R T J L
H L L A O H Y O J T H E F A M E
T A L B C H R O M A T I C A M H
```

Answers on page 191.

ALEXANDRIA OCASIO-CORTEZ

Alexandria Ocasio-Cortez (1989–), often referred to as AOC, was born in the Bronx and attended Boston University, majoring in international relations and economics. During college, AOC interned with Senator Ted Kennedy, where she often helped people affected by discriminatory ICE policies. She worked for Bernie Sanders during his 2016 presidential campaign, and in 2018 she began her own campaign for Congress. She defeated 10-term Congressman Joe Crowley, the fourth most powerful Democrat in the U.S. House of Representatives, in the primary. She went on to win the general election, and at age 29, AOC became the youngest woman to serve in Congress. She has become known for her progressive policies such as the Green New Deal, her outspoken social media presence, and for being a member of the Democratic Socialists of America. She was reelected in 2020.

ALEXANDRIA	ELECTED	POLITICIAN
AOC	GRASSROOTS	PRIMARY
BERNIE SANDERS	GREEN NEW DEAL	PROGRESSIVE
BRONX	HOUSE	PUERTO RICAN
CAMPAIGN	ICE REFORM	SOCIAL MEDIA
CLIMATE	JOE CROWLEY	SOCIALIST
CONGRESS	JUSTICE	THE SQUAD
CRITIC	NEW YORK	TED KENNEDY
DEFEATED	OCASIO-CORTEZ	WOMAN
DEMOCRATIC	OUTSPOKEN	YOUNGEST

```
O W T C Y E L W O R C E O J F W D
C O S S M X N A I C I T I L O P C
A M E G R A S S R O O T S M I E I
S A G R O E D Y P R I M A R Y T T
I N N E F E D E F E A T E D O C I
O S U E E V E N E W Y O R K A E R
C O O N R I M Y A E E T A M I L C
O C Y N E S O D S S S K W E R E N
R I O E C S C E O D E U C F D H G
T A U W I E R N C A L I O N N X I
E L T D H R A N I U E W N H A N A
Z M S E I G T E A Q C I G R X O P
A E P A B O I K L S T I R C E R M
M D O L R R C D I E E O E Z L B A
I I K Z O P M E S H D A S C A O C
L A E I N N J T T T J U S T I C E
C X N A C I R O T R E U P H O U S
```

Answers on page 191.

TAYLOR SWIFT

Taylor Swift (1989–) began playing guitar and writing her own songs at age 12. When she was 14, her family moved from Pennsylvania to Nashville so that she could pursue her music career. She released her first single "Tim McGraw" in 2006, and her album released that year sold more than 5 million copies. In 2010 Swift became the youngest artist to win the Grammy Award for Album of the Year for *Fearless*. Her album *1989*, which featured number-one singles "Shake It Off" and "Blank Space," won Grammys for Album of the Year and Best Pop Vocal Album. Swift's subsequent albums *reputation*, *Lover*, *Folklore*, and *Evermore* achieved commercial success. Her accolades include 11 Grammy Awards (including three Album of the Year wins), 12 Country Music Association Awards, and 32 American Music Awards (the most wins by any artist).

ALBUM OF THE YEAR	FEARLESS	REPUTATION
AWARDS	FOLKLORE	SHAKE IT OFF
BAD BLOOD	GRAMMYS	SINGER
BILLBOARD	GUITAR	SONGWRITER
BLANK SPACE	LOVER	SPARKS FLY
CARDIGAN	MEAN	SPEAK NOW
CATS	MINE	SWIFT
COUNTRY	MUSIC	TAYLOR
CROSSOVER	NASHVILLE	TIM MCGRAW
EVERMORE	POP	WILLOW

```
M U S I C E S O N G W R I T E R
S L G P O E N I M B U D B L O H
T Y O P H U R E V O S S O R C N
I P M W O N K A E P S T A G F O
U S S M E R O M R E V E A O E I
G H D R A Y C M E A Y R L C A T
N A R O M R E V E E E K A A R A
A K A L P T G B H G L P W R L T
S E O Y N N M T N O S O S D E U
H I B A A U F I R K L W L I S P
V T L T E O S E N L I O T G S E
I O L B M C I A I F V A U A L R
L F I U A D L W T E C I G N I S
L F B A D B L O O D T R A W A P
E L O V E R D S P A R K S F L Y
A W A R D S W A R G C M M I T E
```

Answers on page 192.

JANET YELLEN

Janet Yellen (1946–) earned an economics degree from Brown University in 1967 and received her PhD in economics from Yale in 1971. Her impressive résumé includes positions such as an assistant professor at Harvard, an economist with the Federal Reserve Board of Governors, and Chair of President Bill Clinton's Council of Economic Advisors. She served as Chair of the Federal Reserve from 2014 until 2018, becoming the first woman to hold the position. In 2021, Yellen became the first woman to serve as U.S. secretary of the treasury, and the first person in American history to lead the three most powerful economic bodies in the federal government of the United States: the Treasury Department, the Federal Reserve, and the White House Council of Economic Advisers. She holds several honorary degrees and is the recipient of many distinguished awards.

BANK	CLINTON	GOVERNORS	SECRETARY
BIDEN	COUNCIL	INTEREST RATE	SENATE
BOARD	DEMOCRAT		TAXES
BROOKINGS	DEPARTMENT	JANET	TERM
BROWN	ECONOMIC ADVISERS	LEADER	TREASURY
BUSINESS		OBAMA	WAGES
CABINET	EMPLOYMENT	POLICY	YALE
CHAIR	FEDERAL RESERVE	POSITION	YELLEN
		REGULATION	

N O I T I S O P M E D I B Y P S
I T N E M Y O L P M E B A R Y R
E S E C R E T A R Y P M W U A E
V B O A R C L I N T A O N S L S
R C T M R Y I I A B R O I A E I
E H A S E Y C N O B T E N E B V
S A R R G C N E J N M T T R V D
E I C O U I U L I A E A E T S A
R N O N L L O L L R N T R S L C
L W M R A O C E M E T E E E J I
A O E E T P H Y S N A N S X L M
R R D V I J A N E T I D T A E O
E B R O O K I N G S C B R T A N
D L A G N C R A U S E G A W D O
E A O A H C A B I N E T T C E C
F Y B I D E N I S U B M E S R E

Answers on page 192.

STACEY ABRAMS

Stacey Abrams (1973–) started her involvement in politics while in college when she interned at the Environmental Protection Agency and took part in protests surrounding issues of segregation and the Confederate flag. She earned a J.D. from Yale Law School and worked at legal firms after graduation. In 2002, she was appointed deputy city attorney for Atlanta. She served in the Georgia House of Representatives from 2007 until 2017, and became the House minority leader. In 2018 she ran for governor of Georgia, becoming the first Black woman in the U.S. to be a major party's nominee for governor. Although she narrowly lost the election, she remains active in politics. Abrams founded Fair Fight, and helped register at least 800,000 new voters in Georgia ahead of the 2020 election. She is credited with being one of the major forces behind Democrats' wins in Georgia in 2020 and 2021.

ABRAMS	FAIR FIGHT	REPRESENTATIVES
ACCESS	GEORGIA	SENATE
ADVOCATE	GOVERNOR	STACEY
ATLANTA	HOUSE	SUPPRESSION
ATTORNEY	LAW	VOTERS
BALLOT	MINORITY LEADER	VOTING RIGHTS
BIDEN	POLITICS	WINS
BLACK	RACE	YALE
DEMOCRAT	REGISTRATION	

```
T A N O I T A R T S I G E R D A
A E E A Y S R E T O V O R E W D
R L B B A A Y E L A Y O M P E V
T Y I R D L L E W I N O D R T O
S T D A V L A W N R C A R E A C
I I E N O I S S E R P P U S N A
G R N W C A N V A V O T E E E C
E O I B A I O T N A L T A N S C
R N U I T G H O U S E M T T G E
S I H D E R T H G I F R I A F S
Y M D E M O C V A T N A L T A S
E R E D A E L Y T I R O N I M K
C E S T H G I R G N I T O V N C
A E C C A B A L L O T V S E N A
T T B A L L P O L I T I C S U L
S U O H R A B R A M S C A T S B
```

Answers on page 192.

KAMALA HARRIS

Kamala Harris (1964–) was born in Oakland, California, to parents who emigrated from India and Jamaica. After attending Howard University and the University of California's Hastings College of the Law, Harris began a lifetime of public service. She was elected San Francisco district attorney, California attorney general, and won a U.S. Senate seat in 2016. Harris became well-known for her pointed questions during Senate hearings. She declared her candidacy for the 2020 U.S. presidential election on Martin Luther King Jr. Day 2019, but dropped out of the race before the end of the year. Joe Biden announced Harris as his vice presidential running mate and the two were elected in November 2020. Harris is the first female vice president and first Black person and Asian American to hold the position.

ASIAN AMERICAN	GOVERNMENT	OAKLAND
ATTORNEY	HARRIS	PROSECUTOR
BLACK	HASTINGS	QUESTIONING
CALIFORNIA	HEARINGS	REFORM
CIVIL RIGHTS	HOWARD	SAN FRANCISCO
CRIME	JOE BIDEN	SENATOR
DOUG EMHOFF	JUSTICE	SERVICE
ELECTION	KAMALA	VICE PRESIDENT
GENERAL	LAWYER	WOMAN

A I T N E M N R E V O G K A M A
H A R R D N A L K A O E I E G Q
P R O S E C U T O R E N E G Y U
T O Q W N R O T T A R E D K E E
N F F O H M E G U O D R E A N S
E E T M E B D Y F Y A A L M R T
D R C A M Q L I W W J L E A O I
I B A N I A L A O A F B C L T O
S G N I R A E H C L L L T A T N
E C N A C I R E M A N A I S A I
R S T H G I R L I V I C O E H N
P I H A S T I N G S L K N E Y G
E T C R C R I M N E D I B E O J
C S E R V I C E J U S T I C E N
I U U I S E N A T O R E F O R M
V J L S O C S I C N A R F N A S

Answers on page 192.

ANSWERS

ABIGAIL ADAMS
(page 4)

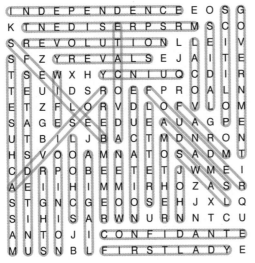

MARGARET FULLER
(page 8)

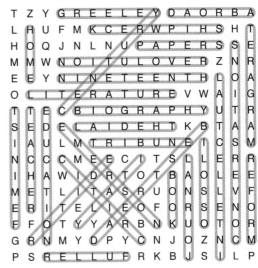

JUDITH SARGENT MURRAY
(page 6)

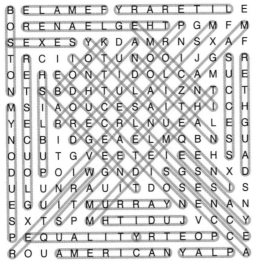

SOJOURNER TRUTH
(page 10)

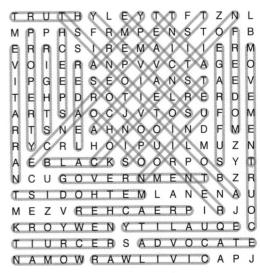

ANSWERS

HARRIET BEECHER STOWE
(page 12)

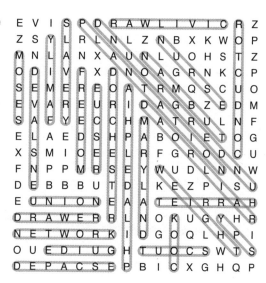

HARRIET TUBMAN
(page 16)

ELIZABETH CADY STANTON
(page 14)

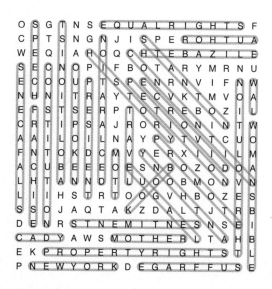

CLARA BARTON
(page 18)

ANSWERS

LOUISA MAY ALCOTT
(page 20)

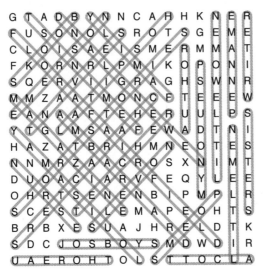

JULIA WARD HOWE
(page 24)

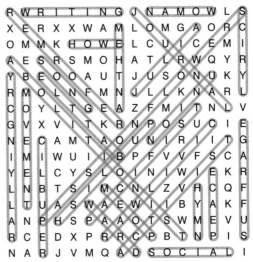

SUSAN B. ANTHONY
(page 22)

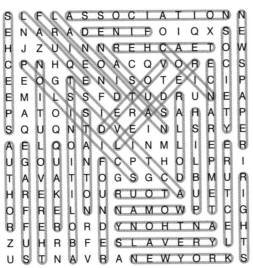

VICTORIA WOODHULL
(page 26)

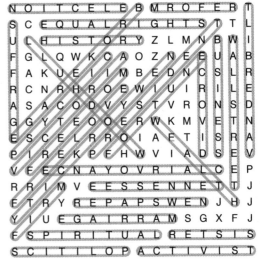

ANSWERS

EMILY DICKINSON
(page 28)

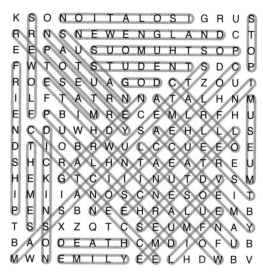

JANE ADDAMS
(page 32)

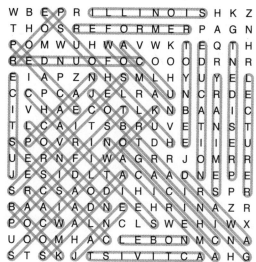

MARY CASSATT
(page 30)

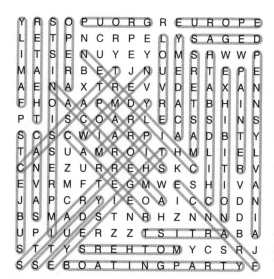

NELLIE BLY
(page 34)

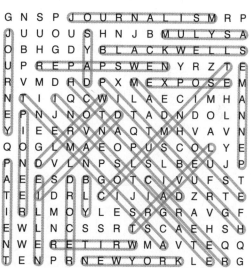

ANSWERS

IDA B. WELLS
(page 36)

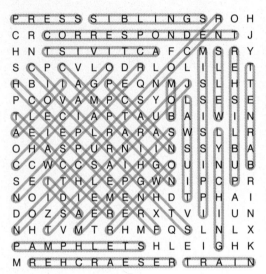

EDITH WHARTON
(page 40)

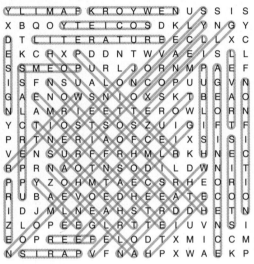

SUSAN LA FLESCHE
(page 38)

MADAM C.J. WALKER
(page 42)

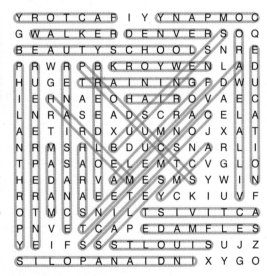

ANSWERS

MARY MCLEOD BETHUNE
(page 44)

MARY PICKFORD
(page 48)

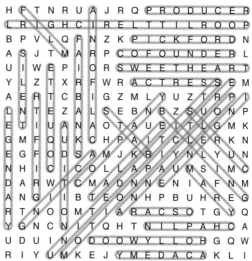

HELEN KELLER
(page 46)

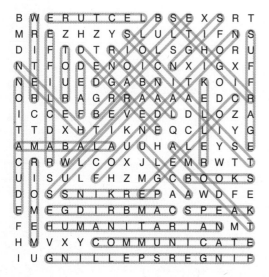

MARGARET SANGER
(page 50)

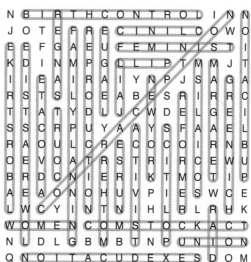

ANSWERS

GEORGIA O'KEEFFE
(page 52)

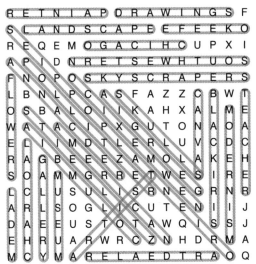

PEARL BUCK
(page 56)

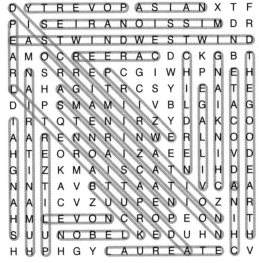

AMELIA EARHART
(page 54)

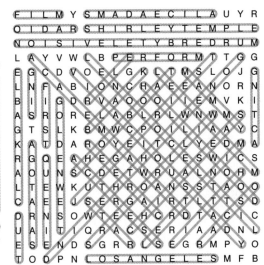

HATTIE MCDANIEL
(page 58)

ANSWERS

ELEANOR ROOSEVELT
(page 60)

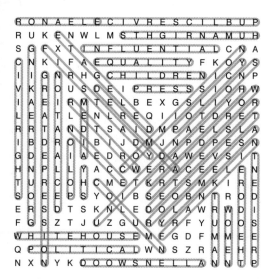

LUCILLE BALL
(page 64)

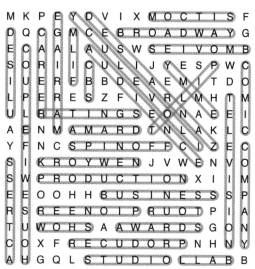

MARGARET CHASE SMITH
(page 62)

RACHEL CARSON
(page 66)

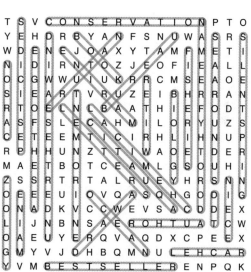

ANSWERS

ELLA FITZGERALD
(page 68)

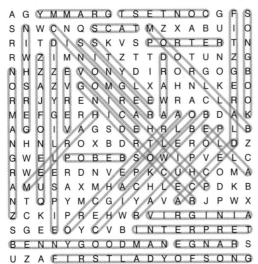

ROSA PARKS
(page 72)

GRACE HOPPER
(page 70)

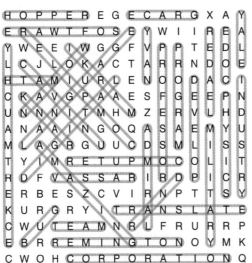

KATHERINE JOHNSON
(page 74)

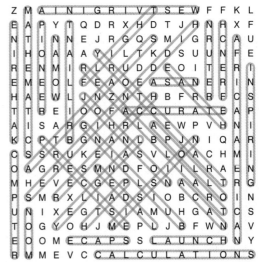

ANSWERS

RUBY BRIDGES
(page 76)

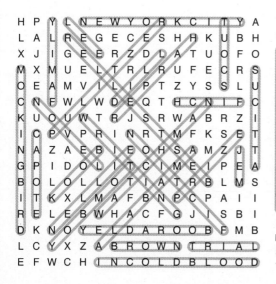

DOLORES HUERTA
(page 80)

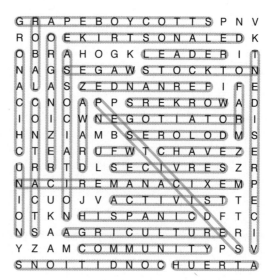

HARPER LEE
(page 78)

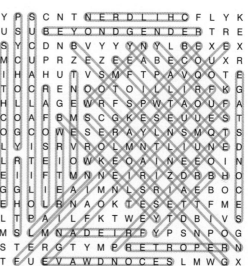

BETTY FRIEDAN
(page 82)

ANSWERS

PATSY MINK
(page 84)

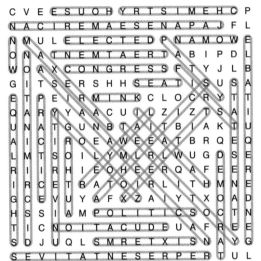

FANNIE LOU HAMER
(page 88)

LADY BIRD JOHNSON
(page 86)

RITA MORENO
(page 90)

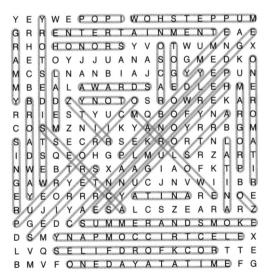

ANSWERS

SHIRLEY CHISHOLM
(page 92)

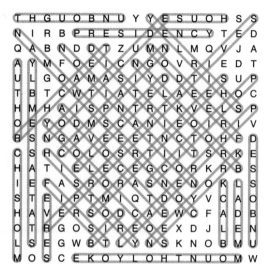

GLORIA STEINEM
(page 96)

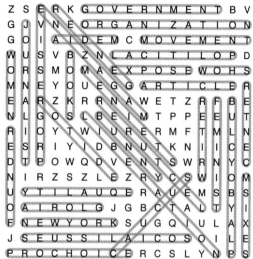

CAROL BURNETT
(page 94)

MAYA ANGELOU
(page 98)

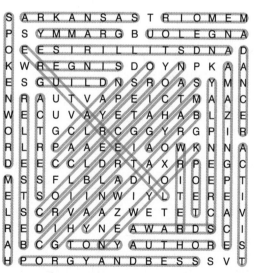

ANSWERS

MARY TYLER MOORE
(page 100)

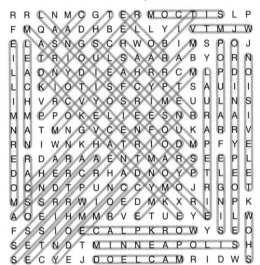

BILLIE JEAN KING
(page 104)

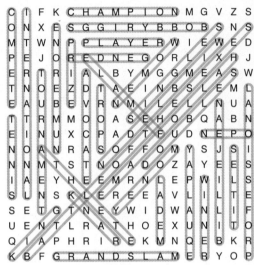

BETTY FORD
(page 102)

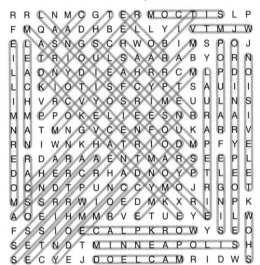

TONI MORRISON
(page 106)

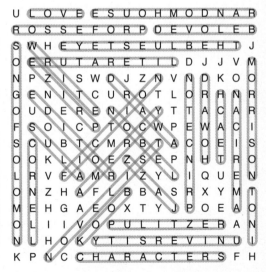

ANSWERS

GERALDINE FERRARO
(page 108)

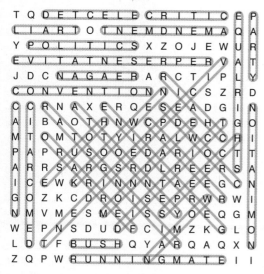

BARBARA WALTERS
(page 112)

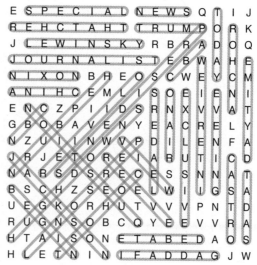

DOLLY PARTON
(page 110)

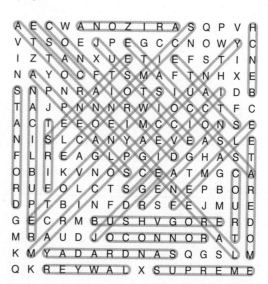

SANDRA DAY O'CONNOR
(page 114)

ANSWERS

JANE FONDA
(page 116)

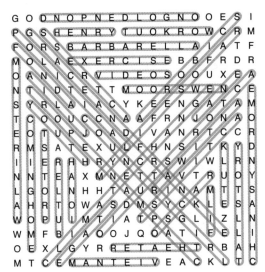

MAYA LIN
(page 120)

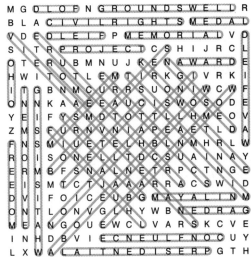

SALLY RIDE
(page 118)

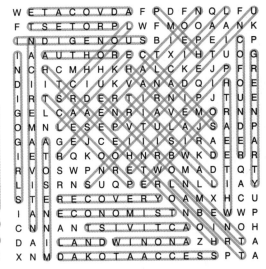

WINONA LADUKE
(page 122)

ANSWERS

ANITA HILL
(page 124)

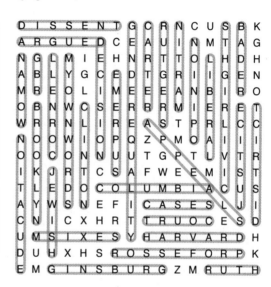

RUTH BADER GINSBURG
(page 128)

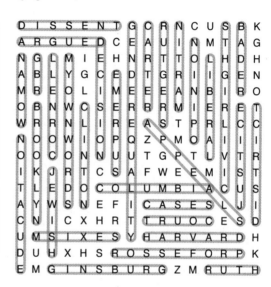

MAE JEMISON
(page 126)

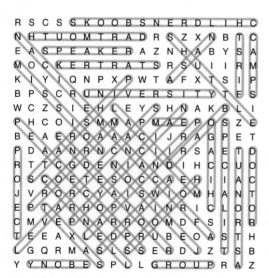

NORA EPHRON
(page 130)

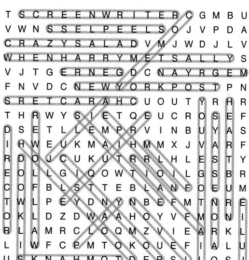

ANSWERS

MADELEINE ALBRIGHT
(page 132)

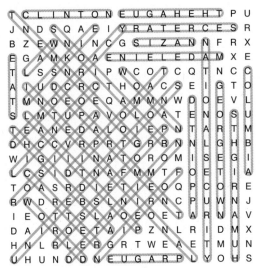

CONDOLEEZZA RICE
(page 136)

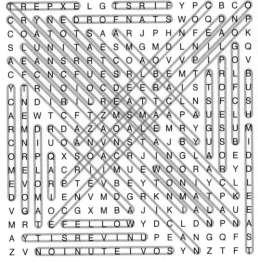

OPRAH WINFREY
(page 134)

KATIE COURIC
(page 138)

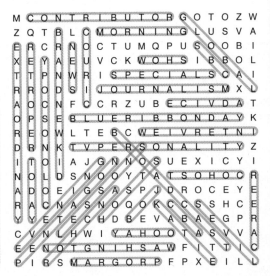

ANSWERS

KATHRYN BIGELOW
(page 140)

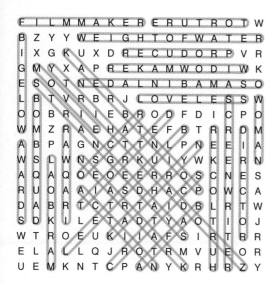

ELLEN DEGENERES
(page 144)

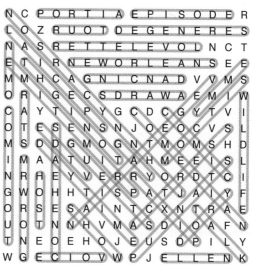

HILLARY CLINTON
(page 142)

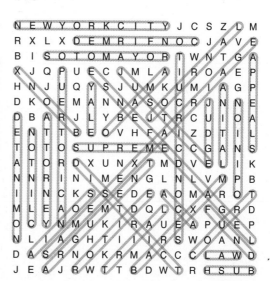

SONIA SOTOMAYOR
(page 146)

ANSWERS

MERYL STREEP
(page 148)

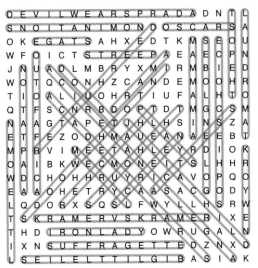

SERENA WILLIAMS
(page 152)

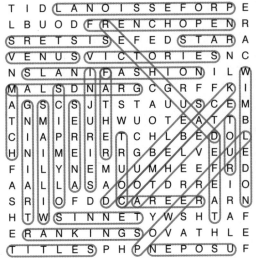

MICHELLE OBAMA
(page 150)

BEYONCÉ
(page 154)

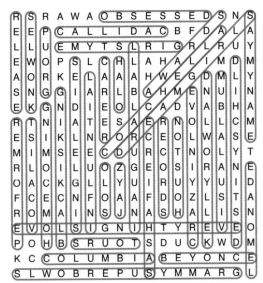

ANSWERS

NANCY PELOSI
(page 156)

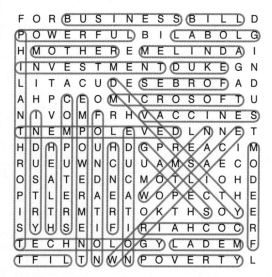

LADY GAGA
(page 160)

MELINDA GATES
(page 158)

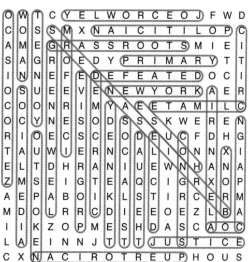

ALEXANDRIA OCASIO-CORTEZ
(page 162)

ANSWERS

TAYLOR SWIFT
(page 164)

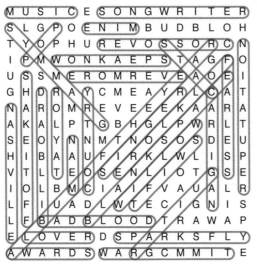

STACEY ABRAMS
(page 168)

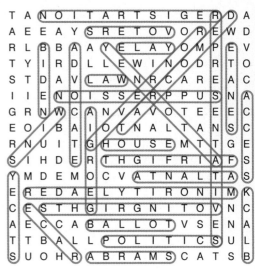

JANET YELLEN
(page 166)

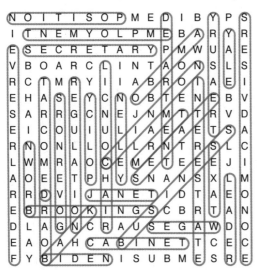

KAMALA HARRIS
(page 170)

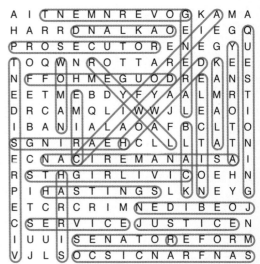

BRAIN GAMES®

GREAT AMERICAN
WOMEN
WORD SEARCH

Publications International, Ltd.

Let's get social!

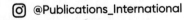 @Publications_International

@PublicationsInternational

@BrainGames.TM

www.pilbooks.com